Running is good sense— and good fun— for everyone!

Not long ago, Dr. Kostrubala was a fat, anxious, discontented psychiatrist. Then he discovered running. He's still a psychiatrist, but everything else in his life has been wonderfully changed.

Running chases the blues, opens huge reservoirs of untapped energy, and offers a host of amazing fringe benefits that will help you completely revitalize your life!

The Joy of Running

Thaddeus Kostrubala, M.D.

PUBLISHED BY POCKET BOOKS NEW YORK

POCKET BOOKS, a division of Simon & Schuster, Inc.
1230 Avenue of the Americas, New York, N.Y. 10020

Published by arrangement with J. B. Lippincott Company
Library of Congress Catalog Card Number: 76-9835

ISBN: 0-671-54340-7

First Pocket Books printing September, 1977

20   19   18   17   16   15   14

POCKET and colophon are registered trademarks
of Simon & Schuster, Inc.

Printed in the U.S.A.

To my wife, Ann Lewis,
and all my children

Acknowledgments

I SHOULD LIKE TO THANK Kathleen Ahner for her constancy, hard work, helpful criticism and support. Without her aid this book could not have been written. David Bradley, my editor at Lippincott, was invaluable for his editorial selection and for guiding me through the labyrinth of moving a book from conception to publication. John Boyer, M.D., and Tom Rice of C.P.R.I. were the ones who helped me begin to run, and, of course, without them my own running and the book would not be here. After that I should like to thank various members of the San Diego Marathon Society, such as Ozzie and Kip Gontang, Eileen Waters and Craig Silberman, the St. Charles School Running Program and the Sisters of Mercy of Burlingame for their support of a health and marathon program in one of their schools. Dr. Al Kreinheder deserves special appreciation for his personal guidance into the realm of analytic psychology. Dr. Stu Brown helped by his cheerful encouragement throughout this process. And most of all I thank my patients and friends from whom I have learned so much of what is in this book.

Author's Note

No TWO HUMANS are exactly alike. We all differ from each other to a greater or lesser degree in one way or another. While the physiological and psychological principles and actions advocated in this book will be more or less true for the majority of readers, any individual reader may be different—you may be different. You may discover that you have to move more slowly to avoid undue aches and pains, or illness. You may discover that the suggested pattern is too slow. There have been people who have died while running. Running is stress, and stress can kill. The program outlined in this book is designed to minimize the stress, and therefore the danger. However, each individual must respect his own physiology, psychology and environment. If you suspect you may have a cardiac problem, or a potential cardiac problem, *consult your physician.* You should, before embarking on this program, have a thorough physical examination and a stress test, especially if you are over thirty. In running, use this book as a general guideline, but be constantly aware of what seems best for you. Feel free to modify patterns to your own needs. But don't give up. The rewards are too great.

Contents

1

The Heart

THE HEART IS A PUMP, a bloody pump. It sits somewhere in the upper middle of me. The statistics show that it is my number-one enemy. I don't have to look out there—outside—for what is to get me; it's right here. A time bomb, 2 inches inside my chest, armed by fat and booze and smoke, pumping, ticking, clogging. Ready to stop.

When people die from a heart attack, they know it. There are those few seconds—ten or so, maybe even thirty—when, after the heart stops, they *know* it has stopped. I wonder what they do, what they think. I wonder if they try to tear away at the chest wall in a feeble attempt to grab at the heart—to give it a squeeze, to make it *go* again. The rest of the body is still alive—the brain still sends its messages to the arms and legs, the nerves still fire, the glands all work—but it doesn't matter; the heart has stopped; all the rest is dependent on it.

Half of the people who have a first attack die from it, most before they can reach a hospital. But it's not always the crushing chest pain and then the coffin. It can be a slow, agonizing cycle of pain, recovery, depression, patch-up jobs—and then another attack moves in. The "recovered" coronary patient is in the midst of the cycle. He has had his attack and—usually by luck alone—he has survived. He is a kind of Lazarus, resurrected. Somewhere between Jesus and Frankenstein. But his heart, his center, his core has been damaged and will never, he believes, be the same. *He* will never be the same. A freak now, he huddles in fear over the hurt. His chest sinks. His chin lowers. His shoulders slump forward. When he moves, he inevitably brings his hands up over his heart. His "recovery" is very temporary; even one of the 50 percent lucky enough to survive his first attack by four weeks has a five times greater chance of dying in the next five years than those who escape that first attack.

There are 1½ million people in the United States who have "survived" a coronary. There are an additional 2 million people with *known* coronary problems—stenosis of a major artery, or angina, or rhythm and conduction defects due to coronary heart disease. There are perhaps an additional 7½ million unknown or asymptomatic cases. This year—every year—700,000 of them will die.

I am a physician. I know these figures. I am over forty years old, and the odds are closer to me than . . . my heart. I have the knowledge of the time bomb within my own body. I have a need to protect myself. One way to protect is to deny. Deny the pump. Deny the statistics. Deny my own vulnerability. If, as I go to sleep, I hear the blood in my ear on the pillow, a swift agonized turn pushes the creeping terror away. My dream is that nothing is different; the common round of my day, rising, shaving, eating, driving, working, talking, sleeping, comforts me. This is the lullaby of reassurance. The knowledge of this killer, with me as his victim, is driven away to the far edges of my mind.

In September, 1971, my family and I arrived in San Diego, having moved from Portland, Maine. Although we didn't admit it to ourselves, something had been wrong with our life in Maine. We had not formed any close friendships. My practice was flourishing, but there wasn't any meaning in it. I blamed it on the weather. In April, with the express purpose of engineering a change, we had sailed a sloop to the Bahamas. We had hoped the experience would draw us closer together—I was forty then—but the attempt had failed, and now I felt my marriage would fail.

Something was terribly amiss with my ability to understand the world about me and the world inside me. This in spite of serious attempts to understand the outside world via science and anthropology, and the inner world by undergoing psychoanalysis and becoming a psychiatrist. My use of science and anthropology produced a kind of cynicism about others and the world. I became increasingly tense. My agitation was converted to work—long hours and multiple involvements with politics, organizations, clinics. I felt some kind of inner hunger, a need I could not seem to fill. I tried with alcohol, overwork, involvement, speeches, money and "things" to satisfy the hunger. I bounced and ricocheted from project to person, searching and not finding anything. I rarely glimpsed any beauty. It was foreign to me. Achievement was my only goal, but I had no purpose; when I asked myself the question "What do you want?" the immediate inner answer was "More." I did not know how to touch, to caress; I grabbed. I did not look; I examined and dissected. I did not hear; I talked. I was at war with the world about me. Nothing unfolded. I was like a hatchet, a sledge hammer: anger, drive, fatigue were the major components in my life.

On the level of a curriculum vitae and *Who's Who* and the social page, I was a successful physician and psychiatrist. I had even been called innovative, charismatic and brilliant. But somehow I was a failure and I knew it. I felt that there was no way out of the path I was on, that there was no alternative to persistence and dogged perseverance, which I mislabeled "courage." Discontent, self-loathing came up from below. Some soul-saving grace, some guardian angel arranged enough vision for me to stir powerful currents of depression. This was an accurate self-appraisal. Alcohol had become my drug of choice. I was tense, fat; and I somehow knew, when I cared to see, that I had lost contact with those things that refresh the soul. At times these feelings would overwhelm me, and the inner voice kept trying to get me to see how distorted I had become. Once while I was flying cross-country, somewhere in the sky in middle America a poem on a scrap of paper came welling upward. The words conveyed tumors, warts and ugliness. That alcohol-infused scrap of poetry showed not only my own ugly self-picture, but had at its core the scuzzy twins of self-pity and paranoia.

And fear. Because I didn't have to think very deeply or develop any insight to realize that I was a prime candidate for a heart attack. I weighed 230 pounds. I was 5 feet 11 inches tall. I drank heavily. I did not exercise; I didn't even take walks. I *never* ran. My blood cholesterol was quite high, and my blood pressure was beginning to rise. According to everything I knew about heart disease, I was in line to have a coronary. The number-one cause of death in men over thirty-five was stalking me. The statistics show that cardiovascular disease, including heart attacks, strokes and other blood-vessel diseases, account for the numbers one, three and four as causes of death. Number two is cancer.

It probably looked like an impulsive act; I asked two of my friends who they felt was the best cardiologist in San Diego. They gave me the name of John Boyer. I had my first examination by him on my forty-second birthday. John's examination was thorough and coldly factual. In addition to the usual physical exam and blood tests, he also gave me a resting electrocardiogram and a stress electrocardiogram. All the tests pointed in the same direction. I was a high-risk normal; I stood a good chance of having a heart attack. When I tried to get the statistics down to a meaningful number for me, I found I faced the problem each of us faces when he tries to place himself on a graph. We always seem to think that we will escape the odds. We'll be at the far, far right of the bell-shaped curve—that coronary will land on someone else's chest, not ours. I could practice self-delusion as well as anyone. So what does a "good chance" of having a coronary mean? Well, it meant to me that if I dared to look at myself without blinking, I could have one any day. I was embarrassed, depressed and frightened, chagrined at my own inability to do even the simplest exercise without getting dizzy and out of breath. As I looked at John— ten years older than I—I was even more embarrassed. In spite of his graying hair he looked fifteen years younger than I. He said that he was beginning a program within a few weeks for patients who had had coronary heart disease. It would entail being retested and then running under supervision, and he recommended that I join the program. If I had any doubt about the seriousness of my condition, it evaporated at that point. I was to be treated along with those men who had survived the dreaded killer. I wasn't a colleague any longer; I was a patient. It was as if I had had a coronary myself. I didn't like *that* idea at all. I especially didn't like the thought of being together with those men whose hearts had already been damaged. I had an odd fear of contamination. Perhaps, in some crazy way, I would "catch" having a coronary. After all, I hadn't had one yet.

I was surprised at John's suggestion. As a psychiatrist, I had not been active in the field of cardiovascular work. I knew there was some progress in the area of cardiovascular surgery, but I had never heard of exercising cardiac patients, and I had been active in medicine my entire life. And during medical school and afterward, I had taken a particular pride in keeping abreast of new developments in medicine.* But here was a treatment pattern, or therapy, I had not heard of before.

In all my previous medical training and experience, I was familiar with two major aspects of coronary heart disease: cause or causes and treatment. As to the first, there was much argument about the relative contribution of diet, stress, obesity, blood pressure, family history, occupation, etc. As for treatment, it was simply to limit the patient's activities and manage him with medication.

So here was John Boyer, M.D., prescribing exercise—specifically, running—as a preventive measure for me, and he was planning to use it as a therapeutic tool in treating men and women who have had coronaries. I asked him about this method and learned that this was a new, but not unknown, technique. Approximately twenty years ago, in the 1950's, Dr. Fred Kasch, then in Illinois, began to experiment gingerly with both normal subjects and cardiacs, by conducting stress tests and then carefully exercising the subjects. His results were exciting. He demonstrated that the human heart was, like any muscle, responsive to progressive, carefully monitored exercise. As the heart responded, it became a better pump. Its strength increased, and apparently its vulnerability to heart disease decreased.

However, this work was not in the mainstream of American medicine. It was also viewed with suspicion and some hostility by other doctors. Fred Kasch was not an M.D. but a Ph.D., an exercise physiologist.

In spite of this reluctance to accept it, the idea did catch on, and physiology laboratories all over the United States began to repeat the work of Dr. Kasch.

___

* Editor's note: Dr. Kostrubala is an $A\Omega A$—Alpha Omega Alpha, which is the honor society of physicians as Phi Beta Kappa is the honor society of undergraduate schools.

Finally, a small group of cardiologists began to do stress testing, and today, in virtually every major city in the United States, one is able to find cardiologists who understand and use stress tests to examine the functioning of the heart. In many places today both cardiacs and high-risk normals can enroll in a carefully monitored, medically run exercise program, such as John Boyer's in San Diego or Jack Scaff's in Honolulu.

But it was all new to me. I still had the old feelings from the past that a coronary was inevitable, and once you had one, you'd had it. I learned, further, that John Boyer had decided to change his habits and his practice several years before I'd met him. He began to work with Fred Kasch, who had moved to San Diego and was a professor at San Diego State University and directed the exercise physiology laboratory. John began to run, too.

The date approached for the program to begin. The first order of business was thorough testing—stress electrocardiogram (ECG), testing of pulmonary function, measurement of body fat. I joked my way through the tests.

A stress ECG is a major tool used by the cardiologist. First electrodes leading to the ECG machine were taped on my chest. A blood-pressure cuff was fastened to one arm above my elbow. And then I was seated on a bicycle, an unusual stationary bicycle that had only one front wheel. I pedaled against a specifically measured resistance, and as I was pedaling, the ECG was recorded on paper and on an oscilloscope. Also my blood pressure was taken and recorded at various intervals throughout the test. John watched the ECG for any signs of abnormality as I began to work my heart. I got sweaty and weak and my legs trembled. It felt like an eternity. The machines kept on, and finally the test was over. I almost passed out. They laid me on a table and kept the measurements going. They had worked my heart to its maximum capacity and looked carefully to see if the electrical activity of the heart indicated any early malfunction. From this stress test I got my "target rate" expressed in the number of beats per 10 seconds. That rate was 75 percent of what my heart could do, and was not to be exceeded. Beyond that level it could be dangerous.

The cardiovascular stress test is an indirect measure of the functioning of the heart. During the test the physician closely watches the ECG for any appearance of abnormal electrical activity. He also watches the pulse rate as it appears on the ECG and the blood pressure. Finally, he observes the patient for any clinical signs of difficulty such as leg or chest pain, a bluish color to the face and so forth. The theoretical maximum goal of each patient is 100 percent of his maximum cardiac output. That means driving the heart to perform at its best possible functioning level. This is usually expressed in a number of beats per minute and is obtained from a table which is derived from the average population as adjusted for age and sex. Clinical experience has shown that exercise at 75 to 80 percent of one's own maximum cardiac output, as expressed in a pulse rate, produces significant beneficial changes in the heart and cardiovascular system. At that rate the heart is oxygenated, and heart damage is not likely to occur. Beyond 80 percent difficulties can arise, such as faulty oxygenation, which can lead to tissue damage, a heart irregularity and even death. When the heart is exercised with an adequate oxygen supply, it is said to be aerobic.

Thus, a well-run cardiovascular stress test provides two important pieces of information. The first is information about what has happened so far to the heart; in subjects with no known heart problems, the test attempts to discover any latent ones. The second is that it provides information specifically relating to the tested individual about a safe rate of exercise. This is expressed in a "target" pulse rate, either for 10 or 15 seconds or for 60 seconds, the full minute.

If the ECG uncovers any abnormality, then the patient should begin his running program under direct medical supervision.

I felt like a freak. A fat freak. The figures all came out as they had in John's office, but with added indictment: I was the fattest of the group—fatter even than those who had had coronaries. I was told to appear with running shorts, sweat suit and sneakers on a Thursday afternoon in October, 1972.

My notion of exercise was "punishment." This idea was directly related to my two years of active duty in the Marine Corps, where exercise was often explicitly used as a form of punishment. Exercise, punishment and pain were all linked together in my mind. But here I was. In my car. Driving to my execution. My wife had packed my gear—lumpy blue sweat outfit, silky-nylon blue shorts, white socks. I felt ludicrous. I was an idiot to dress like that, and even more so to expose myself to ridicule. Others would see me as I "ran." I had seen those fat middle-aged men "run." It was worse than obscene.

I arrived at the high school where the program was set up. A small classroom. A dressing room. A track on a kids' grassy football field. The staff was there. I was greeted. Smiles painted on the landscape of faces. The first duty—to take our own pulse rates. We had all had our stress tests. When we had our stress tests, our maximum cardiac output* was determined on the exercising bicycle. What we were now given was our target rate for 10 seconds—that 75 percent of our maximum cardiac output. This differed for different men according to the status of their hearts. Mine was the number 23 (75 percent of 184, or 138, divided by 6). Exercising at my target rate meant exercising at a rate

---

* The term "maximum cardiac output" used throughout this book is not a technically accurate term. It is a convenient usage to describe the end result of the stress test. The stress test does not directly measure the heart's output of blood as a pump. It measures only the functional aerobic capacity of the individual at the time he takes the test.

that was safe for *me*. In the beginning I was able to maintain that rate for only ten minutes of an hour. The rest of the time I exercised at a lower rate. As the weeks passed, the time spent at my target rate gradually increased so that eventually I was able to run at that rate for the entire hour.

Your own pulse—can you believe how hard it is to take? To take it means to bring to active consciousness the evidence of the time bomb. It means ripping away the comforting barrier of denial. It invites terror. We were being asked to feel, count and relate to the enemy. Many of the men who began could not take their pulses. Their fear was too high. They had to be gently guided, helped and encouraged. It took time. My fingers, trained for years to do this simplest of physician's chores, were now turned against me. But my pride did not allow me to fudge and fumble. I had to face my pulse. I felt like a victim, a fool. I couldn't really fathom my emotions. My hopes didn't even exist.

As I talked with the others in the dressing room, the reality of all the propaganda and statistics hit me. I was a "high-risk normal"; they were "cardiacs." I was a car speeding down a freeway without brakes. They had already crashed. They were back on the road, but they had been wrecked to a greater or lesser degree. I could see the scars that ran down the chests of the ones who had had open-heart surgery. They soon found out that I was a doctor and a psychiatrist, and they openly talked about their experiences. They knew their special place among men. The killer had touched them. They were now more vulnerable than others. They came with heads down, shoulders hunched, moving slowly, often shuffling. Their depression was all too painfully clear to everyone around them. Their hopes, if any, were few.

The setting of the running was supposed to provide reassurance. All the personnel were trained in cardiac resuscitation. They had a portable ECG machine and they would check and recheck us as we ran and walked in a large circle on the grassy field. But that ECG and the portable "crash cart," which was part of the same unit, only served to underscore the seriousness of the business we were about. The crash cart had a portable defibrillator and medications to restore someone who might have a coronary on the field. About two months later, supposedly "into" the program, I went through a period when I would stop at a liquor store on my way to the field and buy a pint of vodka. I would sit and furtively gulp the burning white liquid enough to ease my fear before I ran. I knew it was a dangerous thing to do—drinking constricts the coronary capillaries—but reason wasn't enough. Fear was too great.

The running pattern was quite simple. Each patient was individually shown how to keep at his own target rate for a certain number of minutes per session. The length of time he kept at it depended on the degree of cardiac damage he had sustained. A man who had had a very severe heart attack with consequent severe damage could remain at his target rate from ten to fifteen minutes for many sessions. The running was scheduled for three times per week. All the experimentation with these programs had shown that this was the best minimum. The advantages are not lost from session to session. The physiological changes, which are slow, do take place at that rate.

Before we started that day, John Boyer made a short speech. He said he hoped that this meant for each of us a permanent commitment to a change in life-style. The people who say they have answers seemed crazy to me. Cultists. The descendants of hippies, whom we inherently distrust, or jock types full of loud rah-rah. Candide Frankensteins. I back off. Retreat to the shore. Have another martini, vodka martini (a small compromise—it's less toxic than gin). But John's words came home. I decided that, if I had gone this far, I was going to try. I had no idea then what that decision meant.

My first day at the program I found I could not run 100 yards. By run, I mean a slow, shambling jog. My target rate was exceeded. I puffed. I had to slow down. I had to walk, then run, then walk again.

2

Genus Homo

FROM THE MOST DIM GLIMMERINGS of prehistory through the classical age of Greece and the ages of Roman civic and military power, we hear the clear statement that man's body and soul are related to each other. This is encapsulated in the Latin saying *Mens sana in corpore sano,* "A healthy mind in a healthy body." There seems to have been no question in the perceptions and concepts of our ancestors that physical and mental health were clearly interrelated. But somewhere in our more recent past, we in the Occident have lost this synthesis of body and mind. Today we are left with a troubled way of looking at our states of being, dividing them uncomfortably into the artificial groupings of body and mind. We are forced to grapple with bizarre terms such as "psychosomatic," to spend endless hours attempting to explain the mechanisms of communication between supposedly distinct entities, to hear the arguments of two differing groups, the one devoted to the physical side of man and the other passionately defending the ethereal inviolate temple of his "mind" or "soul."

In the National Museum in Kenya there is a skull which was discovered by Richard Leakey and Bernard Ngeneo in 1972 in the Lake Rudolf area of Africa. It has been identified as a meat-eating species of our own genus. It is called "Skull 1470." Its owner was an upright walking primate. He is our direct ancestor.

As we attempt to search for meaning, our meaning and purpose whether as a species or as an individual, we are intrigued by our history. As children and adults we are often curious about our ancestors, for we seek clues in them as to the sometimes puzzling events in our own lives. Skull 1470 is at least three million years old.

This ancestor was curious in several ways. He walked upright, used primitive tools, did not know the use of fire, had an opposable thumb and binocular vision. He coexisted with another creature who bore a remarkable resemblance to him. This other primate was *Australopithecus*. He also walked erect, had opposable thumbs, used simple tools and had binocular vision.

For all their similarities, however, Leakey has demonstrated that these two primates differed in one important aspect: their femurs were shaped differently. The probable interpretation is that our direct ancestor walked upright permanently, while *Australopithecus*, though capable of walking upright, did so only for brief periods. We say "probable" because all of our information is inferential. We will—and again, probably— never be able to see exactly how we evolved, or how we differed from other creatures that resembled our ancestors. So we must try and guess.

What advantage did walking upright at all times give early man? We must again refer to some of the historic evidence for other possible clues from which we might speculate further.

We do know that the first cities appeared only about

5,000 years ago, and that agriculture was invented or discovered about 10,000 years ago. But just because cities appeared for the first time 5,000 years ago, we cannot assume that the majority of the population was urban, when in fact it has remained rural well into modern times. In addition, prior to the agricultural beginnings of 10,000 years ago, men were hunters and gatherers. Even today there are groups of humans who still live as hunters and gatherers, such as the Tasaday, recently discovered in the Philippines.

Thus, we have two distinct ways of life. The first is the hunting-gathering pattern of life, which involved the majority of our evolution. The second is the sedentary, fixed, urban way of life, a much more recent lifestyle for *Homo sapiens*. If we compare the first cities, dated at 5,000 B.C., to Skull 1470, dated at 3,000,000 B.C., we see that the ratio is 1 to 600. To use a more comprehensible comparison, it is 5 miles to 3000. To travel coast to coast across the United States mainland involves a distance of 3000 miles. Just think of how minute that 5 miles is in relation to the 3000.

During the entire time period from 3,000,000 B.C. to at least the cities of 5,000 B.C., our ancestors were mobile. They walked, hunted, gathered, migrated and probably ran, both in their hunting and at times in fear.

Let us now compare selected examples from what we are learning about man's possible capacity to run.

The Tarahumara Indians in the state of Chihuahua, northern Mexico, are perhaps the world's most remarkable long-distance runners. They live in an area of rugged, mountainous terrain. Visitors and investigators of the Tarahumara have noted an absence of cardiovascular disease. While they can be observed running slowly from place to place, their running is a natural life-style rather than a trained activity. For pleasure and entertainment they run a weekly race of approximately 30 miles in group fashion, and on special occasions they run races as long as 150 miles.

A second example are the Australian aborigines,

known to hunt kangaroo both in groups and, on occasion, alone. The lone Abo may spot a kangaroo and pursue it at a slow jog all day, into the night. The next morning the Abo rises, goes to the kangaroo and kills it. The kangaroo, too stiff to move, is unable to escape or resist attack.

The Hopi Indians are also reported to have run long distances. One group rose before dawn, ran 10 miles to their fields, worshiped at dawn, worked the fields all day and then ran the 10 miles back to their dwellings.

Another vivid example is the eyewitness report of Laurens van der Post in *The Lost World of the Kalahari* (pp. 231–235) that while in his Land-Rover he followed three Bushmen hunters as they closed in on an eland. Although they had run over 20 miles in their pursuit, they were fresh, not at all fatigued at the close of the hunt.

Again, we do not have an explicit answer to our question, only tantalizing hints and possibilities.

In looking for evidence of the first appearance of heart disease in our species, here too we have very little to help us. Even the well-maintained Egyptian mummies offer no clue, as the embalming process entailed removal of their hearts and other viscera. However, a recent discovery in China unearthed a remarkably well-preserved lady from the tomb of a wealthy princess who lived and died over 2,000 years ago. In fact, the Chinese were able to perform a modern autopsy, with the following findings: she had died of a heart attack; she was obviously wealthy, was overweight, had borne children, had type A blood and had died suddenly after eating. There were herbal medicines in the grave with her, cinnamon, magnolia bark and peppercorns, which are prescribed for heart disease by herb doctors in China today.* She was about fifty years of age.

The key factor is that she led a sedentary life. In

* *National Geographic*, May, 1974.

some way she was a prototype for us today, with our affluence and our sedentary, fixed, urbanized life-style.

Is it possible that "natural" man in those three million years of development had an additional physical characteristic keyed invaluably to his survival, and that his ability to cover long distances on foot is precisely that characteristic? Is it possible that man as a species may be a superb, long-distance-running land animal and that he ran in this manner as a daily part of his life as he searched for food, both hunting and gathering?

Today we carry vestiges of an earlier biological past, such as the appendix, which was a functional organ before we became primates. As we develop as an embryo, we see gill slits and other clues to our biological heritage. But what about the effect on the psyche of man? Is it possible that such a long span of years has left an underlying basic structure of inherited characteristics that we are not able to apprehend because of our recent urbanized life-style? Perhaps they lie buried in our unconscious experiences that are denied to us because we are not resonating with that long history we have as mobile man, running man. If they are locked up within us, perhaps there are ways to release these unconscious contents to our benefit.

But before we explore that aspect of man's nature further, it is perhaps instructive to see what we are able to learn about the effects that urbanization produced. The first step was agriculture. This allowed the development of planned leisure time. There then followed the evolution of the class or caste system. The priest astrologers looked to the heavens and saw what they apprehended to be a rigidly fixed, ordered universe. They then translated that concept directly into human terms. The concept was evolved that society itself should be a reflection of the rigid ordering of the gods. The gods gave laws to man, the priests interpreted, the rulers imposed the laws and the goal of the individual in such a society was to bend every effort to conform to that structure. Individuality was actively discouraged and conformity was placed at a high premium. This concept of the individual being subservient to the supraindividual state, even to the point of his own death, is the predominant concept in man, even today. The nation, the company, the institution assumes a greater status than does the individual.

One of the functions of myth and religion in any society is to give the individual a guide into the structure and function of his own internal world. In this way, as we read the myths of ancient Greece, we are able to see the inner soul, or psyche, of the ancient Greeks projected into various myths, dreams, tragedies and comedies. Ideally, this will reflect back onto other members of the society and provide them with some guidelines to understand themselves. In the best of circumstances this process can lead to enlightenment, spiritual enrichment and personal realization. In the ancient East, and today in totalitarian societies, the principle of individuality, or the development of the ego of the individual person, is discouraged, suppressed and if possible even destroyed. The ideal roles of the society, the archetypes of the social order, are instead promoted and extolled. Thus, the individual is programmed to see that the only good role is the one given to him by society. And that society bends its efforts to reward him for that conformity. This ends in an attack on creativity and spontaneity. The creative personality is demolished beneath the juggernaut of an absolutist culture, and individuality disappears. This demolition of the creative personality is perhaps one of the most significant and terrible consequences of our super-industrialized world. We somehow know this and turn to practically anything that will lead us out of this dismal destruction of our individuality. And so we become attracted to Yoga, Zen, new religious concepts, drugs, dietary fads—anything to help us out.

This concept of man enslaved to an idea beyond himself was first broken in ancient Greece. There a new, fresh vision of man came into being. The gods were not absolute. Laws were not fixed and rigid. Man had an opportunity to change his social position. He was not necessarily enslaved. This idea was fragile and was one of the concepts that helped spawn the Golden Age of Greece. It was a unique idea, but perhaps one that was first held by our earlier, free-hunting, running ancestors. In Persia, in the East, the concept of the monolithic state grew and flourished. The ancient Persian Empire threatened the independence of the Greek city-states, attacked the West and emerged victorious, defeating the Greeks and other Europeans and invading as far as the Danube. The battle seemed unequal. The Greeks, obsessed with their newly discovered concepts of gods, laws and man, often fought with each other and could not seem to rally together to stop the marching hordes of men whose views of themselves and the world were so different.

Finally, after prolonged debates, voting and politics, the Greeks formed a confederacy—not a union—and together fought the Persians. The Greek confederates were Athenians. They represented the ten tribes that comprised the Athenian population. Each tribe had a general and the ten of them formed a council. There was an elected eleventh man who was the leader of all. His name was Callimachus. He had been elected the war-ruler of Athens in the year 490 B.C.

It was September. The Persians had landed again. The Persians had enslaved the known world and had been victorious for fifty years. The Athenians had, at best, 10,000 men. The Plataeans, a small city-state, were friends of the Athenians. They had been befriended by the Athenians and came to their aid. Thus were added 1,000 men to the European army. The Spartans were not represented; they had delayed marching, as the Persians landed on the sixth day of the moon and the Spartans would not march until the moon was full. The Persians had 100,000 or more men, and they had cavalry. The Greeks had none.

The Greeks were encamped on the heights above the

Plain of Marathon. The plain below was wet in the fall and provided poor footing for horses. The King of the Persians, Darius, was enraged at the Athenians, for they had dared to remain free and had helped the Ionians, who were enslaved by Persia. According to Herodotus, "He took his bow, shot an arrow into the sky and prayed: 'Oh! Supreme God, grant me that I may avenge myself on the Athenians.'" And he had a servant remind him each day, "Sire, remember the Athenians."

Finally, the Greeks, under the commander Miltiades (in this democratic army the command rotated amongst the generals) launched a surprise attack. Eleven thousand Greeks came down from the hills in a line of spears, heavy on the flanks, the center of the line thin. Usually the Greeks advanced slowly and steadily, but here, a new tactic was born: the Greeks *ran* at the Persians.

The Persians thought them mad, but carnage followed: the Greeks pressed on and won. There were 6,400 Persians dead. The Greeks had lost 192 men. Then one Greek messenger ran the 22 miles from the Plain of Marathon to Athens. When he finally reached Athens, he cried out, "Rejoice, we conquer," and fell dead. That was the first marathon.

In the defeat of the Persians, that contentious spirit of Western man, holding onto the hope of individuality, had won a victory. The Greeks knew the significance of this battle. Usually they took their dead home. At Marathon they buried them in a large burial mound and then erected columns for the ten Athenian tribes with the names of the men of each tribe who had fallen engraved upon them. Six hundred years later, the historian Pausanias could still read the names on the columns. Pausanias said the battlefield was haunted and at night the noise of combat and the snorting of horses could be heard. Some believe today that at midnight, in September, one can still hear the echoes of this most significant battle in the history of the spirit of man.

The ideas of democracy and individuality immediately flowered in Greece. Aeschylus, Greek poet and playwright, actually fought at Marathon. The battle of Marathon launched the brief years known as the Golden Age of Greece when art and ideas flowered.

But ideals of individuality are brittle. The notion of man as an agent of the state or church eventually returned. Time passed and other lands, other men, have had to struggle to retain a hold on that slender thread from the past. The concept of individuality has continued to remain fragile. It is alive but not too well in the modern world. The battle of East and West has lost its geographic features, and creativity and individuality face dangers as terrible as anything in the ancient East, hidden in the seductive trappings of pseudopatriotism, pseudoloyalties or pseudoreligion. This concept of individuality is so difficult to grasp that it has had very limited success and has suffered under the discoveries of science. Darwin abolished any hope that we had been created uniquely by God. Copernicus showed that we were not the center of the universe. Freud claimed that we were unwitting victims of our unconscious. Geneticists claim that we are preprogrammed from the moment of conception, and the social sciences point to the massive influence of our environments, whether they be ghetto or suburbia, on our personality.

Somehow, however, the tracings of individuality have survived. One of the basic ideas of the modern marathon is that each person must ultimately run that race alone. He can, and should, be helped by others in his preparation-training. But in the final analysis he is there alone, an individual, testing himself, finding himself. It is a unique celebration of individuality.

As I train for a marathon and often as I run one, I wonder if in some unknown way I am linked across time to the events of that first marathon. As I have looked even further into the significant differences between these two concepts of East and West, I have found that the concept of individuality has had a history, and one aspect of that history is that of the Grail.

The Grail legend came into being in Europe when society had become oppressive. Today, just as East and West have lost their geographic significance, we have found that we no longer have any fixed boundaries, no clear horizons, no center of hope. We have lost the belief in a crusade of any sort. We are once again in a wasteland.

The Grail legend is important to us, for if we find the Grail, the wasteland is redeemed. And the psychological secret of the Grail is that the wasteland has penetrated our defenses and now resides within us, diffusing boundaries, coloring all with gray smog upon our souls. So to seek the Grail becomes our individual unavoidable task if we are to redeem ourselves.

I found that in spite of my best efforts I was a victim of the fixed, tense, urban, destroying forces of our time. I was headed directly toward a physical death through a heart attack, and a spiritual death had already seized me. The vision of the Grail was gone, and took with it hope and beauty.

3

The First Steps:
Ablutio

THE FIRST SESSION TOOK ONE HOUR, plus the stretching exercises before and after the running. Out of my usual clothing, in the lumpy blue sweats, I felt terribly self-conscious. I didn't want to be there. I didn't want to look at anyone else. My comfortable identity was being unmasked. I felt exposed. I didn't know what to expect of the program. I knew it involved "running," but there was so very little "real" running at all; during the first session I ran only about 5 minutes—the rest of the time was spent stretching, bending, resting—and gasping.

The actual running felt like stumbling. I tried to recall the few times I had run as a boy, but my memory and what I was doing didn't click together. This shamble was a jigsaw-puzzle piece that didn't fit, but it was all over too soon for me to react violently to the gap between what I remembered as me and what I had actually become. I could feel the muscles in my legs. They weren't really sore, but I knew they were there. I could recall my legs being sore and tired from running,

37

or exercising, years ago. This feeling wasn't like that. I had expected to hurt; I figured that one had to "hurt" to change. I thought I hadn't done enough.

The next day went off about the same as all my other workdays. Work and the usual routine. No one besides my wife was aware that I had started anything new, and I didn't want to think about it too much. There was too much I didn't know. It was too soon, too early, to form any opinions. Certainly there wasn't any "hope." There was a slight bit of relief that I had at least started something, but I didn't have any idea at all *what* I had started.

The next running session was on Saturday. The same routine: greetings, pulse taking, exercises, target rates established, run-walking, portable ECG readings. I had many doubts and questions. I wondered if all of this was going to do anything good at all for me. The critical, negative side of me kept popping up. I remembered all the stuff about heart attacks. People who seemed trim and fit had died. I was aware of all sorts of studies and statistics about diets, genetics, fats, cholesterol, digitalis and heart attacks, but no one ever mentioned exercise. I felt I was a gullible fool to be out here: I knew of no proof that exercise, in any form, did any good at all. Maybe Boyer was a quack. Maybe I'd spend these lousy hours running around like a fool and die when I was supposed to die anyway. Besides, what was better, to run around exposing myself like some delayed adolescent, or to sit in a nice comfortable chair sipping Jack Daniels, eating peanuts and talking with someone. The Jack Daniels and peanuts more than came out on top; the comparison didn't even seem fair. I'd look at the people leading the session with the thought in my mind, "You're a charlatan and I'm a fool." But I determined to continue to go to the program. At the end of this session my leg and back muscles were stiff. The total running time was still about 5 to 10 minutes; the rest was walking and stretching exercises.

The sessions continued each Tuesday and Thursday afternoon and Saturday mornings. Tuesday, Thursday, Saturday became a routine. I had become so accustomed to programming myself to a schedule that all I had to do was to set it up in my calendar and I'd be there. I became familiar with the surroundings and the people and I grew less tense and self-conscious. But that inner doubt still didn't stop. It seemed as if I was always asking myself why I was there. I even came to recognize the resistance that welled up in me—it came as a feeling of severely increased fatigue before I started each time. A nap would seem so much better. Or a drink. Or both. Yes, definitely both. Yet the routine finally took hold, and I solved the small problems—but unusual ones for me—of carrying my running stuff off with me in the morning and planning to take underwear and other clothes, if I had to dress up again after running to go back to work, teach a class or meet my wife in town.

One of the small things I noticed was that I was bathing a lot more. I showered and shaved every morning. With this program I added three more showers a week. That added up to about 150 additional showers per year. An odd fact. I suppose it meant I would be cleaner all over but I didn't take that idea seriously. In fact, I didn't even recall thinking I could somehow save energy, soap and money by stopping. I wonder how I missed that association; I would have happily grasped at any excuse for stopping. But the days rolled on and a new routine was added to my life's larger pattern, by sheer attrition and habit.

It wasn't all grind and misery—there were even moments of pleasure. I liked to be outdoors. Everyone was friendly. I didn't experience any "pain"—I found I was stiff in the morning when I first got up, but after my morning shower that seemed to go away. Slowly my resting pulse rate decreased—but so slowly that, if they had not kept a record, I could not have believed it—and I found very gradually that I had to run a bit longer each time to keep my pulse at my target rate of 75 percent of my maximum cardiac output. So I was running more and walking less. My weight did not change much; within the first month of the program I lost about 7 pounds, but there the loss stopped, and I continued to lumber around the field. When I asked the staff about dieting, they told me not to worry about it yet. The message was simple and clear: keep the running pattern. Don't try to change other patterns such as smoking, drinking or eating. I had asked them about these other habits in those first weeks because I expected a "crash" program—diet, no booze, and so on—since most other "health" programs seemed to incorporate these taboos. And I wanted results a lot faster. I was impatient. But it was all external expectation; I didn't really care if I changed any other habits at all, especially those of eating and drinking.

After I had been in the program for a while, I began to feel that my leg muscles had firmed up. One day I felt cocky. It was a nice warm afternoon. The air was gentle and soft. It was like a spring day back in Chicago where I grew up. I'd been at this thing for six weeks, eighteen sessions. That was a lot to me. I began to have stronger memories of childhood. Of high school days. We were running at a high school and we could see the kids, their classrooms. I couldn't identify with them at all. Too much distance in time, temperament and geography. But something penetrated on that day and I felt zippy. As far as I was concerned, I could kind of bunch up my energy, load up all at once, push those muscles and, at least for 50 yards, feel light and young again. I was tired of the slow stumble. I wanted to run just barely touching the earth, moving fast and free, light and nimble. The temptation was against all the advice the staff had given. They had warned us not to sprint, but I figured it was because of the cardiacs. By now, my heart was okay, and anyway 50 yards wouldn't hurt. I got down to the track and took several deep breaths and did that inner tensing, or bunching up, that I recalled doing as a kid. I took off. At the third step, just barely started, I felt something tear in my left lower leg. A snapping sensation occurred first without any pain. But I couldn't bend my left foot. I pulled up, hobbling. Then the pain began. First a very slight dull ache which got worse. I couldn't flex that foot. I hobbled back to the dressing room, told the staff what I'd done. I was chagrined. I'd broken a rule and paid for it.

I had partially torn my left Achilles tendon. Three hours later, in spite of applying ice, my ankle was swollen and the pain was like a medium-bad toothache. I limped when I walked. Instead of improving, I had crippled myself. Here was the perfect excuse to quit. But the effect somehow was the opposite. I was so determined to continue then that I really didn't tell the staff the extent of my pain, and I tried to run on that leg. They stopped me and put me on an exercise bicycle while I pedaled and protected that sore left Achilles tendon. It bled internally and got blue, then green, then yellow. The swelling went down. I went to see a podiatrist and he fitted me with inserts for my shoes. Something in that injury triggered some resolving mechanism. I became angry, angry with myself. I determined I would heal and run again. I bought an exercise bicycle and rode at home at my target rate. I didn't get depressed. I just got angry. "It," whatever that was, wasn't going to get me. I kept going to the sessions and rode their bike there. I was afraid to break the pattern. Habit, I knew, could help me continue.

I couldn't run for three weeks. When I got back on the track, I had to be careful to keep from injuring the left leg. I used ice after running to reduce the pain, swelling and tenderness. Slowly I overcame the injury, and one day I was able to run a mile nonstop. I was elated, I weighed about 210 pounds and I must have looked like a rumbling, sweating tank, but I had made one mile. I was so pleased with myself. A whole damn mile! I knew, maybe, that somewhere in my past I had run that far before, but no one had ever measured it. I couldn't recall it at all. It was a first for me. I guess it took me fifteen minutes. I didn't care. I had gone the whole way nonstop. I came home and told Ann, and we had a small celebration. I looked at how far a mile was when I drove in the car. That's a long way! The next session I tried to go a mile but found that I couldn't do it. I was disappointed. I was experiencing the normal developmental pattern or training pattern, but I didn't realize it. It was a week before I was able to repeat my mile.

At about this point in the program, somewhere between two and three months, I became aware of two things. The first was the feeling that I was not at all fatigued after an hour of this type of running-walking. Strangely, at the end of the session I had a sense of energy and a kind of pleasure. It wasn't connected to any achievement factor that I could see, for I would feel that way even if I had not fulfilled my own preset expectations—such as running a mile. I did not understand this odd shift in feeling. It was a sense of well-being, a sense of energy. I wasn't at all tired. In fact I was more talkative than usual. I looked forward to going home and then doing something. In the past, at the end of the day I would come home and be fatigued. Sometimes I'd feel better after dinner. The fatigue of the day appeared cumulative. That's what was "normal": it was logical. It was even more logical to be fatigued after running at the end of the day. But the experience was against all that logic. Something had happened. The slow exercise had stimulated, or triggered, a new sense of energy. Now when I came home to Ann, I was bright and fresh and eager to do things. She was surprised and pleased. I seemed to be more cheerful.

The second discovery was that the other men felt the same way. We discussed it in the dressing room. Who would have thought that running would give us more energy! We expected to be fatigued—but instead we were refreshed. And this feeling was common to us all, whether we were cardiacs or high-risk normals. By this time the group of us had grown closer together. As a physician I knew the risks they ran, how close to death they were. My respect for them mounted each day. I saw that they, too, were having this running "high." We had found something together, and it brought me closer to them. I felt a great respect for their determination and courage. Here was a direct reward for the running, a feeling I could enjoy and anticipate. One of the clear features was that it didn't have a thing to do with competition. We were all of us products of our competitive male culture, but we were in a setting where competition could mean serious harm and pain, as I had experienced. Or death. We were all doing something, for want of a better word, called running. At our own rates. And we all felt better. (I believe there is a connection—a direct one—between the non-competitive aspect and the positive aspects of the group process, but this same phenomenon has been experienced by many who run alone, providing, of course, that they run in this particular way. We can run alone and still be bullishly competitive and destroy this feeling.) At about this same time several of the men reported that their wives told them they were less depressed. They were cheerful when they got home. They were more active. There were indirect implications that sexual interest was increased. Their interest in the world about them increased. They were less preoccupied with themselves and were less withdrawn.

I checked this out with Ann. She said she felt that I, too, was less depressed. It is an odd fact that, in many types of depression, the person who is depressed does not *know* he is depressed—he becomes used to that state of being. But when I examined my feelings, I found that I *was* less depressed. My burdening constellation of oppressive emotional baggage fell apart as I advanced into the process. After running for forty-five minutes or an hour at 75 percent of my maximum cardiac output, I found that I was incapable of putting together that mosaic of misery. Obviously, I was in touch with some natural cleansing process. For a while I thought that I was "losing my mind." I began forgetting things and seemed to recall irrelevant material. I didn't function as well as I did before. I now know I actually was, in some odd way, "losing my mind." I'm glad that I have "lost" that particular mind-set. But I also know that it is ready to return at any time. That part of me has not gone away. He, it, is an evil god. I think I understand him. I have a hunch he is not unknown to other men in this time and age. He is sponsored by our machines, our odd beliefs about the world and ourselves. And he kills his worshipers, sacrifices them through heart disease, strokes, suicide, alcoholism. His victims lie all about us.

My professional curiosity was aroused. I decided to ask the wives to gather for a small group meeting. They agreed. They all supported the finding that their husbands were less depressed. As I continued to talk with the men in the dressing room and on the field, and as the occasional group meetings with their wives developed, I began to see that they, the men, were like survivors. There is a survivor syndrome. Survivors of wrecks, planes and cars. Of divorces. Of deaths. Of illness. They had survived an attack on their hearts. Like survivors they were at first stunned, then thankful, then fearful of a recurrence. They had a story to tell—if someone would listen. I began to listen to these survivors and their wives. I avoided the generalizations in the medical literature, the scientific studies. In college I had majored in anthropology; now I was an anthropologist once again, presented with that delight of all anthropologists, a new tribe. I listened and—in spite of myself—learned. All the men's stories had a focus on the heart attack itself. They had to chew over and over the personal meaning of those events. They had almost met their deaths. They escaped. They were survivors. Why, why? Why were they struck down? What were their sins? At first I had trouble listening. The images I had of myself dying of a heart attack returned. I was hearing, face to face—or perhaps heart to heart—how the killer operated. I had cared for coronary patients in medical school and in my internship, and as a psychiatrist I was supposed to be a trained listener, but I had never heard stories like these, about such a personal killer. He was horrible. He struck from within.

As we talked, I shifted in and out of being repossessed by the terror and fear to the old clinical pattern. The "clinical" is the viewpoint of the scientist, the objective observer. The distant. It is safe. It is a hiding place and an especially good one for doctors. I bet some physicians don't let go of this peculiar special defense even at the moment of death. I went in and out, from the terror to the clinical, and slowly the extreme polarity weakened. I was able to experience both feelings, or postures, and combine them. I both felt and observed. And from this new position I began to see the enormous toll this killer takes. I became convinced that something was terribly wrong. We were not *meant* to break down this way. Lives were not meant to be torn apart at such productive times. Fear, fear of our own bodies, should not be part of our lives. But this was precisely what had happened to all of these men around me. They focused on the moment when it happened. The killer struck at all times, all places; on the beach, driving a car, in bed, making love, after dinner. Often it first appeared as indigestion. One episode I heard of sticks in my mind. A forty-five-year-old man at home got up to go to the bathroom. He fell near the center of the living-room floor. His wife heard him fall. So did his twenty-year-old son. They found him lying there. At night. One light on. He was dark blue. Not breathing. They didn't know what to do and stood in a frozen tableau for several minutes. He began to breathe. The son ran to the telephone to call. To call—who? The police. When they arrived with oxygen, the victim was awake and breathing. He was lucky. Many die in those few moments. The heart stops. With luck it will start again. With help, which includes oxygen, or air, and external cardiac massage, the chances are better for it restarting. But most people don't know what to do.

As this particular tribe of cardiacs talked on, they all began to trace certain dominant themes in their lives. There were patterns of tension; of job pressures, financial worries, sexual inadequacies and anger—at an unknown factor, out there, outside themselves, that they knew had conspired somehow to remove hope from their lives and allow them to slide slowly into labyrinths of despair. Not everyone fitted the full picture, but the themes resounded.

I remembered my father. He was born in Poland and came to Chicago at age ten. He learned the American culture well. He first became a dentist, then a physician, and finally a plastic surgeon. He acculturated perfectly. He worked long hard hours, smoked a pack of Camels a day, was highly driven, successful and competitive. When he exercised at all, it was a mimic of the tension at his work. He even said that when a man retires he will die, and he never wanted to retire. But he did retire, at sixty-five. Six months later he had a coronary, but survived with a pacemaker. In another year he was dead from cancer.

As I continued to run and ask questions of myself and these patients, certain patterns emerged. Or perhaps they were questions. For example, why did someone who played tennis regularly and seemed fit have a serious coronary when exercise was supposed to grant some sort of immunity? The difference seemed to be in the type of exercise. In tennis, as in most other exercise, the heart works hard, but only off and on. There are spurts of hard work followed by periods of less work. On a graph it would appear like a zigzag (see Figure 1). The peaks are when the tennis player is working hard. The dips are when he rests, ready to serve or waiting to receive the serve.

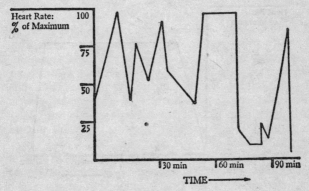

Figure 1

The pattern of running we were doing was entirely different. We were aiming for a pattern like the one shown in Figure 2. Not one of the men who had had a coronary had exercised with this particular pattern.

I began to search the medical and sports literature. I found that there were very few sports that automatically accomplished this pattern. Those sports that did were long-distance running, long-distance swimming and rowing.

I also read that some men who had had coronaries have been famous runners. I also learned that as of 1974 Paavo Nurmi was dead of a coronary. He no longer ran; he had become morose, bitter and often depressed. He also had had several earlier heart attacks. Also, as I read the sports literature I found the old American theme once again. Compete. Compete

against distance, against time. Paavo Nurmi was recalled as one of the most passionately competitive

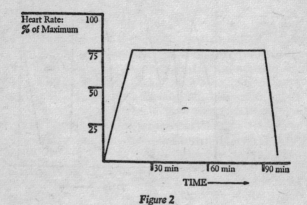

Figure 2

runners who ever lived.* There were only a few references to ways of running other than racing. And in the
sports literature, these were described in derogatory
terms: "philosophical runners," "Zen runners," "hobby
runners." The "real men" had to compete—against
distance, against the clock, against each other, against
themselves. If you operated with these criteria, then
you qualified as a "man." It seemed as if we were
caught in a cultural net of competition, tension, false
values and despair. Using this approach to understanding, having a heart attack seemed one of the "done"
things. A coronary was the new badge of courage, the
medal of honor for keeping one's nose to the cultural
grindstone. And if death intervened, then there was a

---

* There is no record of Paavo Nurmi's ever having completed a marathon.

release from what might be viewed as an impossible trap. Call it retirement.

The weeks passed. I returned to the routine of Tuesday, Thursday and Saturday. I found that, if I had to be out of town on any of those days, I felt that I *should* run, and I did. I recall one time running slowly around the roads surrounding the Milwaukee airport. I was carrying my running stuff with me now if I went away anywhere. I found the other men did it too. On the weekends, especially on nice days at the beach, I would try to do a little bit of running. I was still fat and I felt pretty sheepish as other men and women seemed to fly past me. I'd take my pulse frequently and see what I could do. I can recall trying to go along by running twenty steps, then walking twenty. Run twenty, walk twenty, run twenty, walk twenty. Then I cut it to walk ten to see how my pulse would go. If it went up too high, I'd cut back to twenty. If it was okay, I'd keep at run twenty, walk ten. I was intrigued by how this walk-run pattern slowly allowed me to run longer and longer and walk less and less. I continued to feel and relate more to the other men in the program. The time for my first retesting occurred. This was three months after the beginning of the program. As it approached, I wondered if the ECG would show any difference. I knew I felt better, but my weight was about the same, still over 200 pounds. I had not changed any of my eating, drinking or work patterns.

The retesting day arrived. I was going to have my second stress test. I went through the same procedure. I recalled the first time I was tested. It was only a fifteen-minute test, but I had thought it would never end. I hurt at the end. I was dizzy. My heart pounded. This time I was puzzled. The experience didn't match my previous one. It didn't hurt. I felt no sense of accomplishment. I figured something was wrong. I thought I had been improperly tested. The bicycle must have been set at a much lower load. It actually was the same load, but after three months of running I wasn't dizzy or tired; my heart didn't even get up to its target rate. They showed me the results on paper, the ECG, pulse tracings and blood-pressure recordings. They compared the results of three months before and of today. It was hard for me to believe the marked improvement. I now had two pieces of "evidence" going for me. There were the facts, figures and numbers right in front of me. But more important to me was the subjective feeling of the retesting. I stared at the bike. Slowly a slight edge of hope dawned on my inner horizon. I was changing. My heart and blood vessels had started to adjust to the slow, steady pattern. Changes were occurring. And they happened from the inside out. As I looked at myself in the mirror, I was still fat. But some leg muscles seemed to be obtaining some structure, some definition. As far as I could see in the mirror I was the same, but I knew I felt differently. I had some hope. It was working.

At first I didn't want to run alone. I was used to the group. However, some inner question had got hold of me and I wanted to see where it led me. I felt as if I was slowly breaking away from the pattern the others had established. I felt group and staff pressure to remain within the larger group, but I again pursued that inner question. It seemed to say, "What is going on? Is this change for real? What is the end point? Is there an end point? Where are you?" I found I wasn't afraid of my heart any longer. I knew my safe limits. I checked my pulse frequently, and as long as I was within my target rate, I knew I was safe. And so I went on, slowly running longer and longer times. My fears about my heart were now replaced by curiosity. I continued to experience that sense of well-being, that "high" after running.

Gradually I found I was running alone. I was meeting at the same time as the other men, but my length of run at my target rate was longer than theirs. I also kept track of the distances I was running. I wanted to go for 3 miles without stopping.

I recall the day I did the first 3 miles. It was an unusual day for San Diego. It was late January and there was a cool rain. Instead of going indoors to run I stayed outside. My sweat clothing got soaked—but I continued to run. I began to realize that something "clicked" together that day. I was able to make the 3 miles. When I finished, I was elated. Three miles! My God, that was an unbelievable distance.

I was glowing like a kid who's won some super-special trophy. I told everybody. I guess I was telling everyone else because I couldn't believe it myself. Somehow, if I told them, it would really be real. Running that 3 miles in the rain remains with me as one of the major beautiful memories in my life. The cool rain, my fully soaked sweat clothing and the surprise of being able to do it was like a surprise birthday party when you're a kid. It was very close to what I wanted to feel when I tore my left Achilles tendon. It was graduation and an inner straightening of my back. The process of change which had been "out there" was now in me. It was a discovery that held high hope and future surprises.

4

How to Do It: Exercise, Shoes, Pain and Other Stuff

DEATH FROM CORONARY HEART DISEASE is the number-one killer in our nation. In fact it's epidemic. In San Diego County the number-two killer is cancer, but numbers three and four are related to cardiovascular problems, such as strokes and clots that plug up the arteries to various organs like the kidneys. So, take one, three and four and you've got a really giant number one. When I give a lecture and think about these statistics, I realize I'm talking to the potential victims, sitting right there in front of me. I have seen them in the intensive-care units where all the horrid machinery of modern medicine tries to keep them alive. They lie there intubated, drugged, ECG's blipping. And a lot of them die anyway. I suppose as you read this you somehow figure it won't get to you.

Of all the ways to die, one of the least logical is via a heart attack. The heart is designed to be the toughest part of us. It should not be our number-one enemy. And yet it is.

As a species we are probably the best long-distance

runners in the animal world. We have had to survive for more than three million years by running, to hunt and to compete with our near-human cousins, like the australopithecenes. But now it seems like we've trapped ourselves. We've gone from agriculture to cities and now we are probably declining biologically. We've come so far away from our origins that we feel justified in poisoning our planet and ourselves. The only time we see similar behavior in animals is when we have put them into markedly abnormal situations such as zoos; then they become bizarre. And we humans are stuck in a poorly run zoo of our own making. We call it a city. We have become sedentary, flabby and inert. We stuff ourselves and then finally we reap the poetic justice we deserve: our own hearts strike out at us from within and we die. Seven hundred thousand of us every year.

Of course effects of the crazy zoo aren't directed solely toward the cardiovascular system. We have become physically ugly as well. Our men have flabby bellies and women carry saddlebags of "cellulite" (i.e., fat) around their hips. Obesity is crippling and insidious. And we feel the cure for all of this is to take more pills, more drugs. In fact, one major dominant theme in American psychiatry today is the frantic search for various pills to control our moods. They are searching for "safe" pills for control of depression and to promote euphoria. I can see that wonderful future now. Each medicine cabinet would have in it a series of pills, maybe color-coded. Bright yellow for euphoria, deep blue to go to sleep, violet for meditation, electric blue for a hallucinatory trip and red for eroticism. And, of course, other pills to take away potential ill effects. We could experiment each night. Every morning take a yellow to go to work, then a violet and red for a pleasant evening and then a blue to go to sleep. A perfect chemical day. We are halfway to this perfect future right now. Currently we are obsessed with things. The right house, the right spouse, the right car, the right job. We keep juggling and shuffling in the hopes of happiness. And as we whirl around in this merry-go-round of nonsense, we've forgotten and abused our bodies and our souls.

Why should you run? First of all who are you? If you are a male, of any age, but especially after age thirty, there is a damn good reason: you are a number-one target for coronary disease. If you are overweight and sedentary, that ups the risk. If you are black the risk is greater, as the effects of prejudice and frustration have been turned into high blood pressure, another high-risk factor. So begin from fear. Why die when you can live? Is it a macho or Russian roulette thing? Are you afraid to be identified as afraid? I know some people who seem to smoke for the same reason. It seems to be their final defiance. It's a sense of anger. Okay. Run because you're angry. Run because you've been duped and disenfranchised from a meaningful life. Perhaps you bought the sales slogan from the culture that if you work hard and achieve, get good grades, diplomas, money or whatever, you will be happy. If you are, that's fine. Then run from fear of losing all the nice things you've got. If you're a woman, maybe you'll run to show men what you can do. Women are great long-distance runners. You might do it for health or aesthetic reasons. Or from frustration and anger. It is awful to be a woman in this culture and be fat and out of condition. Perhaps you should run, at least in the beginning, out of a sense of personal rebellion. It's time to take some action against the forces that impinge upon you. There is a way to fight back. All you have to do is run three hours a week, on three days separated from each other, for one hour each time at 75 percent of your maximum cardiac output. I realize that most people don't know what their maximum cardiac output means, and I recall how I myself used to hate running. I wasn't able to do it alone, I needed help. And so, I've tried to outline the steps that I think work.

The first step is commitment. Decide that you are going to do it. This is in your own head or soul or belly—wherever your seat of commitment happens to live. It might happen in various ways. It was fear that moved me. Some people don't like to huff and puff as they climb stairs. Others look in the mirror and are repelled by what they see. It doesn't matter how it goes for you, that inner step is number one. The next step is to block out those three hours. Somehow time seems to gobble us up. I never feel that I have enough time to do much of anything, and almost everyone I know in this day and age feels the same way. We do, however, seem able to schedule our jobs, meals, baths, tooth-brushing, school and sleep. Those are pretty regular activities and somehow I get them done on a regular basis. Try this the same way. Examine your personal calendar—your personal week. Find those three hours. If it's at all possible, I think it's better to run in the morning. The reason for this preference is the increased energy that occurs after one of these runs. At times, when I have run in the late afternoon or early evening, I've found, and so have others, that it is difficult to go to sleep at the usual hour. You are full of energy and active. Perhaps that energy and activity may suit some particular personal preference and you can adjust your running to your own needs. It doesn't hurt to experiment a little with yourself.

The next step is to consult your physician. Don't ask him if you *should* run; he'll probably tell you no. Ask him if you *can* run. You should have periodic checkups anyway. Do not be dissuaded if your doctor tells you running is bad for you; make him tell you exactly what it is about your physical condition that makes running harmful to you. If there is something, you need not give up the idea of running, but you may need to do it in a medically supervised program.

EQUIPMENT

The most important piece of equipment is your footgear. When you first begin with the slow, gentle, walking-jogging pattern, use the tennis shoes you have or whatever you want to use. Then, after a couple of weeks, go to a sporting-goods store and buy a good pair of running shoes, such as Nikes, Pumas or Adidas. It took me a year to find the type and brand that best suit me. There were some rotten moments when I discovered that the shoes I'd bought really didn't fit my style or my feet. Your shoes should be one-half size too large when you try them on. You should be able to get the width of your thumb between the front of your big toe and the shoe because your foot swells when running, and you need the space. The cost of a good pair of running shoes averages approximately $15 to $25. Buy a glue gun to keep the soles of your shoes in continual good repair. They cost from $5 to $12 and slowly drip hot melted glue from a front nozzle. Apply this to the soles and also to the heels of your running shoes. Don't let the heels of your shoes get run down. Keep them flat with layers of glue.

When I first started running, I wore socks and had a lot of blisters and bloody worn areas. I decided to experiment and went sockless but smeared my feet with Bag Balm. This is a commercial veterinary product for cows' udders. It's like Vaseline. At first it felt greasy and repulsive—but it served to prevent blisters. Now I don't have to use socks *or* Bag Balm, and all goes quite well; my feet have adjusted and the blisters are gone. If you do get blisters or blackened toenails, don't do anything about them. Let the blisters burst themselves. But keep your feet clean, and if there is any sign of infection at all, go see your podiatrist.

Your next items of equipment are your clothing. I prefer nylon shorts and a cotton T-shirt. I brag a lot, so these shirts are usually marathon T-shirts I've won at various marathons. I feel that you should always wear something very light in color or with high visibility, such as reflective orange. I don't wear a jock strap; my jockey-type underwear seems better. It's always easier to take clothing off than to get cold and not have anything to get warm. So sweat clothing is usually in order. When I do training runs, I usually wear a white nylon waterproof jacket with a sweat shirt underneath and a T-shirt beneath that. If I get too hot I begin to strip. I also wear a knit cap like a watch cap in the Navy when it's cold. I've found that my forehead gets too cold and my frontal sinuses react and I get a sinus headache. The cap when pulled down to my eyebrows prevents this chilling and the sinus headache. Some women run in their bathing suits. If it gets too hot, they are able to take off their outer clothing.

When beginning to run longer distances, men often have a problem with their nipples. The T-shirt rubs the nipples and irritates them, and sometimes this causes bleeding. To protect the nipples, put some big Band-Aids over them or use Vaseline or A&D ointment on them. In fact, Vaseline or A&D ointment is useful wherever skin surfaces rub together, such as the upper thigh, the upper arm near the armpit and the buttocks. It's lifesaving if you have hemorrhoids: if you do, use it liberally in and around the anus.

A couple of other items that may help are a pair of gloves, a flashlight and a stick. The gloves are to keep your hands warm, the stick is to defend against dogs by pointing it at them, and the flashlight is of use at dusk or predawn to let car drivers know you are there.

EATING

It isn't advisable to eat a meal of any size prior to a run. It will just sit there and not get digested and only contribute to excess weight. There are some curious effects of running on the gastrointestinal tract. Most people have a decreased appetite after running, and it's advisable to follow your feelings. Don't load up with food, but be certain to take in several glasses of water after a run. A good rule is to drink two to three glasses of water before a run and two to three after a run. You'll sweat and urinate a lot, but you need water in your cells to allow them to work correctly; to move the enzymes around and to begin to shake loose all the toxins of a sedentary life. There is also a peculiar effect on the bowels. Frequent, loose or watery stools are not uncommon and not really uncomfortable, because there isn't any cramping. The loose-stool syndrome doesn't seem to last for more than a few days. It appears to precede a weight loss and may be the way the body is preparing for the change.

Little, if any, research is being done in this area. At any rate, don't worry about it. Another symptom is night sweats. Again, they are not constant and do go away. If your loose stools and night sweats last for more than a week, go see your doctor. I trust by now that your doctor will be a runner, too, because the first advice that most nonrunning doctors give to their running patients is to stop running. But if you're stuck with a sedentary doctor and you're afraid to go, I'd suggest you alter your diet. For the diarrhea, cut down on the roughage such as raw vegetables. And add one-half cup of nonhydrogenated peanut butter per day. Night sweats, if really persistent, can be a symptom of some serious disease such as tuberculosis; so if they persist, go and see your doctor anyway. But have him prove to you that you have TB or something else before you stop the running.

It is a good idea to take certain fluids before a run, such as ample amounts of water. Orange and tomato juice are also good sources of electrolytes. Runners have many different preferences regarding fluids. Dr. Tom Bassler, a pathologist and supermarathoner from the Los Angeles area, ran the Maui Marathon in 1974 drinking beer the whole way. (He finished, but was a bit tipsy at the end.) Other runners treat alcohol as if it were the devil incarnate. The crucial point is to be certain to take a lot of fluid and to remain well hydrated all the way. That way all your cells can function and do all those marvelous things that help you lead a better and longer life. Cells that are dehydrated cannot function. So keep the fluids going. Try and drink while you are running.

PHYSICAL PREPARATION

Anyone over age thirty should have a maximum stress test and a good physical examination. After you have made your appointment, you might have to wait a week or two before you can see your physician and have the stress test. This does not mean you have to wait until then to begin doing something to help yourself. You can, with safety, begin to walk slowly for an hour three times a week. In addition you can do the stretching exercises in this chapter. When you begin by this walking and stretching aspect, you will start the necessarily gradual process of conditioning your muscles. Find the number for your target pulse rate from Table I at the end of this chapter, and practice taking your own pulse (Table III). Do not under any circumstances exceed your target number before your exam and stress test. Don't worry if it's below the number. That's fine; it means you're probably safe. Above all, do not run or jog. Just walk. Swing your arms, breathe deeply. Enjoy the scenery. Start taking your vitamins and especially respect the climate. Be especially careful of excessive heat or cold. Don't overstress yourself either way and dress appropriately. Then, when you see your doctor and take your stress test, you will have begun. It's important to activate yourself and do something with your early determination. It's disheartening to sit and wait.

If a person has an abnormal ECG, he should run in a medically oriented program with appropriate monitoring. Realize how dangerous heart disease happens to be. There is no possible way you can tell whether the person next to you is about to pop off dead from a coronary—worse, you can't tell that about yourself. Let's suppose you have had the stress test. The laboratory will give you a pulse rate that reflects 75 percent of your maximum cardiac output. As you begin your program of stretching, walking and jogging, start taking your pulse. Keep it within that maximum target. For example, at one time my target number was 23. That meant that at any time when I was running, my pulse rate, within 10 seconds, should be 23. If it's 22 or 24, that's pretty close and no need to worry. But if it's 20, I'm not getting significant beneficial change in my cardiovascular system, and if it's 28, it is possibly dangerous.

Prior to every run it is very important to do stretching exercises. Slow long-distance running puts a particular stress and strain on a series of special muscle groups. The basic effect is shortening of these muscles with resultant stiffness. In order to reduce the stiffness and possible injury, slow stretching is very important. I use a particular series of exercises. It doesn't take longer than five minutes to do the entire group. The critical thing to remember about these stretching exercises is that they should be done slowly with concentrated attention on stretching the muscles and tendons. Never "bounce" through, into or during one of these exercises. A "bounce" can set up a reflex response just like the patellar knee jerk and the muscle and tendon end up shortened, not stretched. Here are the exercises I use. I've found that if I don't vary them, but go through the series the same way—i.e., in the same sequence every time—I don't have to think about them and I can concentrate on the stretching aspect.

Stretching Exercises

1. *Torso Twist.* Do it slowly, three to the left and three to the right, or a total of three full rotations. Stand

with your feet apart and arms horizontal. Turn your head and fix your visual attention on the tip of your middle finger, right hand. Then slowly turn to the right with the right arm going back. Keep looking at the tip of that finger. Your torso will twist and, as you slowly force your right arm around to the back, you'll be able to feel the muscles in your torso stretch out. Force it to the point where your eyes are strained in trying to look to the right to follow your fingertip. Then slowly rotate back to center position and fix eyes on the tip of the left middle finger and force your torso all the way over to the left. During all this, keep your feet firmly planted. Do not let your heels come off the ground.

2. *Side Slide.* Feet apart, right arm touching the outside of the right leg, left arm up over your head. Bend to the right slowly, slowly, keeping your hand sliding down your leg. Go over as far as you can. Then come up the leg, sliding slowly until you are erect. Then do the same thing on the left side: left hand on the left leg, right arm over the head and again, slowly slide down the left side. When you are bent over to the right, you should feel the pull on your left side. When to the left, the pull is on the right side. Again, slowly, no bouncing, keep both feet planted firmly on the ground. Do this three times on each side.

3. *Body Rotation.* Hands on hips. Bend forward and to the left and rotate the body from the hips, going to the left and then forward, then right, then back up. Back to the left. Do not bend backward. When you come up, come up straight. Do three to the left and three to the right. Again, slowly, slowly. Feel the stretching.

4. *Forward Bend.* Feet apart comfortably, just let yourself lean forward from the hips. Do not try to force yourself to touch your toes. Let your upper body hang forward. Keep your knees slightly bent. Be certain to let your head hang forward. Do this for a count of thirty seconds. Some people, usually women, are quite flexible in this exercise and are able to get their hands to the ground. If you are doing that, bend your elbows

so that you are getting the stretch effect on your lower back. In other words, do not touch the ground with your hands. Your upper body weight is all you should use. Do not try to force yourself down, or to bounce. When you come up, come up slowly. You may have a brief "blackout" as your blood pressure readjusts itself.

5. *Achilles Stretch.* Place your left leg forward a comfortable, large step in front of you. Make certain both feet are aligned in a straight line. Watch out that the back foot isn't turned out like a duck's. Never let your right heel up from the ground. Now bend your left knee. Do it slowly and feel the pull behind your right knee and along the back of your right leg. Do it slowly, don't bounce. Feel the pull and stretch. It may even hurt a little. Keep the heel on the ground. Then reverse with the other foot forward. Do each foot forward three times.

6. *Inside Leg Pull.* Feet very wide apart, about as far as you can get them. Then, keeping your left foot in complete contact with the ground, put your weight over to the right and bend your right knee. You should feel a pull on the inside of your left leg. Slowly, don't bounce, feel the pull. Repeat and do the same on the other side. Do each side three times.

7. *Knee-Chest.* Put both hands around your right knee and pull it up to your chest. Keep your back straight as you do this. Try to pull it up into your right armpit. Do the same thing on the left side. Each side three times. Do them all slowly.

Those are the basic seven stretching exercises. There are many others that are very helpful, such as stretching for the sky, hugging your knees to your chest while rolling on your back, and sit-ups with your knees bent and your arms on your chest like an Egyptian mummy. In this last one someone will have to hold your feet down. The critical thing is to do all of these slowly, with rhythm and concentration on stretching.

WHERE TO RUN

Run where it pleases you most. A soft even surface such as grass is easiest on your feet. But if you have been sedentary for many years as I had been, it's probably best to run on a track. The surface is smooth and it's good to avoid twisted ankles. Also, the beginner should concentrate on his target pulse rate, his bodily feelings, and so on. A track is usually a good place because it's so naturally dull. As you go round and round, it is easier to turn your mind's eye within.

Well, now we're ready to run. So let's begin. Remember these points of style: keep your wrists below your waist level, drop them lower going up a hill. Pretend you are still a four-legged creature and that your arms are running too, and that the tip of your middle finger is the tip of the hoof. Think of yourself as an animal, run on all fours but upright. Change pace, lope, canter, gallop, trot. Keep your head and shoulders even. Watch your shadow when the sun or street lights are behind you, don't let your shadow bob up and down. Land on your heels and roll on your foot. Move your hands, bend your elbows in motion, don't move your shoulders much. Try to see yourself. Think of yourself being looked at. Perform for yourself. Perform for someone else. Don't try to look flashy or fancy; try to look easy and comfortable. Think of someone you saw running who looked graceful and easy and try to look like that. Above all, do not clench your fists. A clenched fist makes me think of a clenched heart and clenched coronary vessels. Let your hands be open and free. Let your image of yourself running carry you gracefully along. Go slowly, don't get competitive or overly tired. If you even think of it, stop and take your pulse. From the tables in this book, or your own stress test, you will know that you are safe. Keep your feet close to the ground. Land on your heels and roll across your foot. Let your weight fall on your foot directly under you. Take shorter steps than you think. Keep your shoulders above your hips, your hips over your feet. Try to keep your head up and set straight on your shoulders. Don't stare straight ahead, look around a lot. Pretend you're hunting or searching like your prehistoric ancestors. Shrug your shoulders. Run a different way for ten steps, maybe more on the sides of your feet, more on the toes. Let your arms dangle for a while. Wriggle your toes while you run. Try breathing in rhythm with your steps, then forget about it.

A lot of people ask me about how to breathe. I guess that question comes from a lot of nonsense about breathing. My usual answer is that in the Northern Hemisphere you should breathe in your right nostril and out of your left, and vice versa in the Southern Hemisphere. Such nonsense usually breaks the spell with a chuckle. But someone took me seriously the other day, and as we ran I "demonstrated" the technique with such idiotic facial distortions that he caught on. There is one very serious admonition about breathing, and that is regarding conversation. You should always be able to talk, to hold a conversation. If you can converse, you are aerobic, not anaerobic. The anaerobic state can be dangerous and could lead to a heart attack. Aerobic, as noted in Chapter 1, means that your blood is sufficiently oxygenated to allow the respiratory systems that work muscle tissue to operate. We can work our muscles so that they operate without sufficient oxygen. This is the anaerobic state, and it's dangerous. If you run too fast or too hard, the heart musculature may not get enough oxygen to function properly and this could precipitate a heart attack, or coronary. Or the heart may not have developed adequate coronary blood vessels to sustain a heavy work load. Then the portion of the heart that is unsupplied is starved for oxygen and actually dies. This can set up an abnormal reaction in the nerve conduction pattern of the heart, leading to an arrhythmia. This can be serious enough to cause the heart to flutter. If that fluttering, called fibrillation, occurs in the ventricles, then death will occur because the heart cannot pump blood through them any longer. This is one reason why all this running must be done within the safe range of 75 to 80 percent of your maximum cardiac output. At that rate you are always aerobic and the necessary changes in your heart and other blood vessels are able to take place with safety. People who have already had heart attacks should be trained to run in a medically supervised program, with all the necessary equipment and trained people around to help them in the event that their hearts get into trouble. For example, there have been people who have had their hearts go into fibrillation while in such a program. They received prompt medical attention and their hearts were restarted. In other words, they did not die and were able to continue the program and continue the process of their own rehabilitation.

Do not neglect breathing. A trick which may only be pure suggestion but which seems to work is to "whoof" out all the air in your lungs every once in a while. It seems to ease things up. Maybe it only changes the pace of breathing. Tuck your butt up and under. Let your hips swing and open out your stride. Keep running but reach for the sky. Lift yourself up. Run over the ground, not on the ground. Find a hill, get fearful of it and then go master it. When you go up the hill, lower your head slightly and drop your arms. Make the hill a joy. When coming down the hill, do not bring your arms up; don't windmill around the place. Keep your arms down and your feet close to the ground. Land with your knees bent. Let your gravity carry you. Make your steps shorter. Keep in control. If you want to speed up, pretend someone has a hook in your knees and is pulling them forward exactly parallel to the ground. You'll go faster then and it will be easier.

When you run, you will encounter pain. It's important to have some understanding about pain. First of all, pain is real. It's real simply because you feel it. There isn't any way to make pain objective. However, we try to do so in order to measure the effectiveness of our "pain" drugs. A bright light of a specific power and radius is focused on the forehead of a subject at a specific distance, and we then ask him where it hurts. So you see, even our best efforts end up as the subjective report of some individual. Therefore, there isn't any fake or imaginary pain. It's all yours, and when you tell me you have a pain, I believe you fully. So believe yourself. But realize that pain is a complicated business.

For example, when a matador is gored in the bullring, he has no pain; pain comes later, if he lives. There is no pain in combat. Men have lost arms and legs without pain—it comes later. If you ever happen on an auto accident and if the victims are conscious, they may talk and be lucid, not in pain; but they may be dying from fractures and internal injuries—the pain comes later when they get to the emergency room. These reactions are normal and natural. Now let's discuss other types of pain. I know an internist who had coronary chest pain for a whole day before he decided to get help. And he did have a heart attack. Fortunately, he survived. This pain can be like a clenched fist at the chest. It sometimes radiates down the left arm, sometimes in the neck and sometimes into the right arm. It is also described as a pressure or heavy feeling on the chest, like someone sitting on your chest.

If you ever have such pain or anything like it, then be certain to check it out immediately. At times it seems like persistent indigestion, a stuffed-up feeling up high in your stomach or way low in your throat. I hope you never have pain like this. If you ever do have such a pain, get medical help immediately.

There are "usual" pains you'll experience as a runner. First of all, realize you have not been using your bodily machinery for quite some time. For example, when I began running, I ran like a duck. My footprints in the sand looked like a duck's waddle. Now my toes practically point straight ahead, but it took two years for my body to realign itself. Had I tried to straighten it out immediately, I would probably have broken something. It takes time to get straightened out and you should allow for time. Meanwhile, the joints are rusty and the bodily oiling machinery is creaky and, as it gets going, you will have some pain. There will be knee aches, foot aches, odd burning pain in your lower back, peculiar aches in your neck. I remember very vividly running on the beach during the first year when I thought I heard someone behind me. I turned. No one there. I listened again and I heard a distinct *click, click, click* in rhythm with my own steps. I was mystified but then located the sound in my own neck! Was I scared! I thought of getting paralyzed. What the hell was it? Well, I still don't know. It was probably some arthritis in my neck that has now gone away. I didn't feel any pain but kept running and slowly rotated my head.

Perhaps the most common pain is the one in the side. A side stitch. The best treatment for that one is to pay close attention to it—that is, focus your attention on the pain and keep running. It will go away. If you want to do something different, try changing your stride, or blow all the air out of your lungs, or yell, or sing a song. Belly breathing also helps. Head pain isn't dangerous unless you get dizzy. If you get dizzy while running, stop until it clears up fully. It could be an early symptom of heat exhaustion or heat stroke. Get to know your aches and pains. Find out what relieves them and you will find they will get less and less troublesome. There is a kind of small subjective pride in these small pains. When I get up in the morning, I'm stiff. It's nice; it reminds me that I've done my running.

These aches and pains are a good reason to associate yourself with other runners. In meeting with them you can talk about your various pains and all the things people use to fool around with them. Some use ice as an excellent pain reliever. During my first year of running, I kept Styrofoam coffee cups filled with water in the freezer. Then when I'd sit down after a run and have a sore Achilles tendon or a sore knee, I'd hold the cup and put the ice directly on the aching part. Soon it would get numb as I rubbed the ice back and forth across the area. The Styrofoam allowed me to hold the ice without freezing my fingers. The cold causes the blood vessels to constrict, and then they overreact afterward—dilate, carry off the toxic products, increase local circulation in that area and also bring in the needed enzymes, minerals, proteins and vitamins. Some people love hot whirlpool baths and others insist on turtleneck sweaters to keep colds away. For a long time I wore heavy wool socks to bed, as my feet seemed cold. It worked, and I haven't needed them for quite a while. Sounds eccentric, doesn't it? I don't even know if it worked just because I imagined it worked or not. In fact I don't care. I'm only interested in the fact that it worked and I'm eager to learn what works for others. Become familiar with your body and how it works for you. And one of the significant messages your body sends to your brain is pain. Don't be afraid of it. Think about it, discover its meaning for you. One of the most dangerous things you can do is to ignore your pain. This doesn't mean pampering yourself or going to the other extreme and injuring yourself. Your own response to your pain can tell you a great deal about your own personality.

Women seem to run with greater ease than men. Their style is easy. The natural style of most twelve-to-fourteen-year-old girls is almost perfect. They do not clench their fists. They don't fight through their stride. They roll their feet, their pelvises move. They look at ease and ready to play; in fact, they are playing. Is all this because they have not been the victim of male cultural expectation—that of competition? I don't know. I do know that women often have special questions about running, even though it is as natural for them as for men. All the women I've talked to have said that running does not make menstrual cramps worse, but they may run more slowly during their period. A few have said that their cramps have become less over several months as they ran. I can't tell if that would have occurred to them without running. Cramps are most often caused by a combination of factors, the physical and the psychological. The physical is the engorgement or swelling of pelvic blood vessels which supply the uterus, ovaries, Fallopian tubes and upper vagina prior to menstruation. The psychological usually has to do with the way the girl was taught to expect to feel. If her mother went to bed each month and complained of pain, the young girl could be expected to fear her own menstrual cycle and magnify a discomfort to a pain. After that the pattern gets repeated until the girl experiences pain.

Running might alter these two factors in the following way. In the area of the physical engorgement, it is possible that the increased blood flow throughout the entire body might alter the hemodynamic aspects in the woman's pelvic area. This is all inferential; we cannot see these changes directly. In addition, with loss of fluid through sweating, there is dehydration and, therefore, a total reduction in body water which also might have an effect. The psychological factors are much easier to see and demonstrate. For example, an accurate history of how the girl's mother felt about menstruation will often be a clue as to the early attitudes transmitted to that girl. Also, this can be the same attitude toward all forms of pain. At times, women are virtually crippled by this psychological set. They avoid all forms of discomfort for they experience it as pain. When a woman is helped to realize that a pain in her side while running, like a sore muscle, is not going to harm her seriously, she may then be able to reexamine her attitudes toward other forms of pain. She may then reexamine the pain of her periods with this new perspective.

Some women hold onto more fluid in the latter half of each period than others. The water retention is secondary to the hormonal changes that occur. It is lost when menstruation occurs. Running does affect water retention. A woman runner can learn to control her bodily water. A long run will dehydrate her if she restricts her fluids. But, in fact, I would advise against doing this as I think it might be risky. She might expose herself to heat exhaustion or heat stroke. The better thing to do would be to take a lot of fluid and to see what happens. Some women report that running makes their menstrual cycle more regular. Running does not seem to affect the heaviness of the menstrual flow, but, again, there is no real research. Many women feel sluggish before and during menstruation and are apt to avoid strenuous exercise. If they do run, it should clearly relieve the sensation of fatigue and sluggishness. However, feelings like that may be a part of the natural pattern of that woman, and she should respect her natural pattern. In other words, try the running and see if it does benefit you and has no adverse effects. If it does help, then it's okay, but if not, then just lie back for a few days. Women are sometimes irritable just before their menstrual flow. Running does help. This irritability is probably secondary to fluid retention. However, there are other factors which produce tension or irritability besides those which are purely hormonal or physiological. Running has a direct effect on those aspects that contribute to tension and irritability that are primarily psychological.

I have not noticed any problems due to running with women who are on the pill. But I have noticed that some women experience pain and discomfort with the IUD and that this will probably be accentuated by running. If you feel intense discomfort, consult your obstetrician. It may be necessary to have the IUD removed. In the matter of running during pregnancy, I would defer to your obstetrician. Some women have difficulty maintaining a pregnancy and they should be very careful regarding their physical activity through the entire pregnancy, but I have seen women run, and run long distances, without any difficulty, up to their ninth month. Those women who run appear to have normal deliveries. Running tones and aids the pelvic muscles.

Other specifically female-oriented questions concern equipment, such as a bra. Is there a best style, and so forth? A good bra that holds the breasts firmly is helpful. Bouncing breasts can be painful. And if a girl's breasts are overlarge, they can act as a pendulum force on the upper body, which then becomes difficult for the girl to handle. So a bra that holds the breasts firmly is important. I have a subjective impression that breasts that are too large get smaller as a girl runs. Several women have told me that this does happen to them—that the first place they lose weight is in their breasts.

One error in style I've noticed in women who begin to run is that they hold their hands too high. It's as if they attempt to compensate for the swinging of their upper torso by holding their arms high and crossing them in front of themselves as they run. This only sets up a further problem in style. The best advice to give them is to encourage them to lower their arms so their wrists are below their waist level.

Some women seem to be natural long-distance runners. Eileen Waters, for example, is the world champion for women in the 50-mile distance for 1973 and 1974. When she runs that distance, she gets faster the longer she runs. Most men gradually get slower, the longer the distance. The current theory is that women are better able to convert body-fat deposit stores to energy than men. There is a lot of interest in this area right now, and some men are trying to convert themselves to "fat burners." They are doing this by a combination of long runs and fasting. One of the strangest things I've noticed in women runners is the itching-legs phenomenon, and so far I've only seen it in women. This occurs usually within the first half hour of running, when a woman's legs will begin to itch, and the skin is distinctly reddened on their legs at that time. It's more common in beginning runners and disappears over the next several months of running. I don't know what causes it; in fact I don't even have a good theory to help explain it. One postulate is that women have a greater layer of subcutaneous fat than men and that may, somehow, be related.

Women have been brainwashed to keep them from being physically active. The overt and covert attitudes of the culture have kept women from entering various forms of athletics. In running, for example, the first woman to enter the Boston Marathon was Kathy Switzer, in 1967. Officials examining the entry form didn't notice she was a woman, and when the race started and the truth dawned, a marathon official ran onto the field and tried to push her off. He failed and she finished. Ever since then, more women have entered marathons. And their records are constantly getting better. In 1974 Jacki Hansen ran the marathon in 2:43:54, which was the world's record for women. In October, 1975, she bettered her own record by completing a marathon in 2:38, again maintaining the women's world record. At present there is only a thirty minute difference between the world records of men and women; I predict that women's records in long-distance running will continue to improve and someday may even surpass those of men.

To quote Jacki Hansen from an article in *Runner's World* in April, 1975: "I suppose I ran for all the fringe benefits of being in shape and feeling healthy. Now I'm actually afraid to get out of shape. All those fringe benefits are nice, but they're not the complete reason I run. Why I run comes from within me. It is something I feel I have to do, something I like doing best, and I feel best when I'm doing it." I've heard a lot of reasons from women as to why they run. Many of them revolve around concepts such as health, being physically in tune, feeling fit, play, beauty, movement, freedom, grace.

In contrast, many men, including myself, began from fear; fear of dying from a coronary. I've also noticed women seem more at ease with themselves, smile more often and more easily pace themselves than men. But that again may be a cultural influence; by contrast, men are expected to be grim, drive themselves and look pained. I've seen seven-year-old girls finish a marathon and a sixty-year-old woman running along the beach. Women marathoners seem to do best at around age thirty to thirty-two. That's also true of men.

Many women hesitate to run because they've seen some women athletes who have funny, extra-large muscles. They worry that running will do that to them. Slow long-distance running will not do that. There are basically two types of muscle groups. The first is called the white motor neuron unit. Those muscles are big and bulky, have few blood vessels, have large nerve ennervations and tire quickly. Men get these by lifting the heaviest weight they can manage for sets of six to eight repetitions. The other type is the red motor neuron unit. It is composed of thin, graceful muscles. The nerve supplying it is thin and it has many blood vessels. It is designed for long repetition and develops when a muscle is used many hundreds of times with a light load—as in slow long-distance running. The total bodily changes I've noticed in most women is that they begin to look thin all over. Their legs begin to develop definition in shape and they begin to lose the fat deposits around their hips, upper legs and upper arms.

Women usually develop a distinct facial flush while running. There is an increase in the blood flow to the surface of the skin in their faces. Many have told me it helped clear up acne and other minor dermatologic problems. There is another change that occurs in some women. Their facial features seem to become more distinct as they lose their facial subcutaneous fat. This doesn't happen only in women; it happens in some men.

This shifting of fat produces an aesthetic sense of mobility to one's face. For example, after one long run I came home and my wife told me to look in the mirror. My cheeks were hollow, my eyes sunken and my skin seemed drawn. Four hours later that was all gone. I also know of a runner who had lost so much facial fat when he returned from the 50-mile run that his dog didn't recognize him.

These stories are to underscore the point that with appropriate training slow long-distance running has an unusual effect on fat metabolism and distribution. As for myself, I still have a bit of a buffalo hump. That is a deposit of fat high up on my back just below the nape of my neck. Before, I had a really prominent ugly bulge up there. Now it is almost gone. My posture was never too good (in fact, I used to think I was a Neanderthaler), but it now seems improved because that fat-deposit area is disappearing. I've watched that happen to other men and women as well. Currently I've got my eye on a girl who is running. She has just started. At first she looked terribly ungainly and lumpy. She's been at it now for three months and some of the oddly placed bumps and lumps are going away. She is much more graceful. It's really nice to see that happen. One of the saddest problems that women runners face has nothing to do with either physiology or psychology. They are afraid of all the cracks and comments that people, particularly men, make. It's hard to know what to do about this. I suppose it depends on your own style of handling idiots. I've got two stories to tell that may help.

The first is about a demure young woman who was very shy. She started to run and became proficient. She used to bear the quips in silence. Finally, one sunny Sunday morning a guy with a beer belly was watering his lawn. As she went by he said (with typical inanity), "Hey, you runnin' a little bit?" She answered, "Yes, I've just finished ten miles."

The second story is about one of our marathoning

ladies. Out on a workout, she came across a group of marines, in a pack, who were being selected to become D.I.'s. She had finished about 8 miles. They were just beginning to run. As she ran past they decided, about 110 of them, to run with her. Naturally they went huffy-puffy-clenched-fists, and she sped up a bit to stay with the front bunch. Slowly they all faded away, dropping off one by one. During the whole run she chatted away with them. Finally, when they had all dropped behind, she turned around and ran back the 6 miles to where she had met them at first, passing them once again. I don't know if it's coincidence or not, but the very next Sunday a marine officer appeared at the Marathon Clinic and asked if other marines, including women marines, could join us. Now these women were already past the first stages of running and had overcome the years of prejudice. It's easier if you start with a friend, or a group. The moral support and the conversation help a lot.

When my wife, Ann, started to run, she was quite frightened to run alone. She did not like running down the various roads near our house. She knew she didn't look like a runner, and on a couple of occasions men in cars would offer to give her a lift. Now this doesn't happen to the woman runner who is recognized by those around her as a runner. It probably has to do with speed, style, movement and other factors. So she began to run with a girl friend. This added support and reduced their fear, and they encouraged each other. Running with a partner helps overcome a natural reluctance on the part of a beginner. Even if you are an experienced runner, it helps to establish a social or group aspect to your running. Find a friend who runs and see if a group of people, of approximately equal ability, can meet at a convenient time to run together. This is usually quite hard to do on a daily basis, as our work and personal schedules seldom allow for such flexibility. Here in San Diego I meet with the San Diego Marathon Clinic on Sunday mornings. There we find our friends, and since we are divided into beginners, intermediates and advanced, we are able to choose which group to run with. For example, one man who has run twenty-two marathons had the flu a couple of weeks and he was pleased to walk-run with the beginners. As we meet, we decide how much we would like to run that day, join that group and take off.

Perhaps you are not fortunate enough to have a marathon clinic or a track club easily available to you. Or you may want to form your own running group before getting involved with more experienced runners.

See if you can find at least one or two other people who want to run. If any of you are over thirty, be certain to get your stress test. Have a preliminary, nonrunning meeting and decide on the best time for everyone. Take your pulses, check out the stretching exercises, get your running gear arranged.

Let's say there are six of you. Meet at someone's house, perhaps at seven in the morning on Sunday. Take your pulses again, do your stretching exercises. Bring orange juice and beer as a reward for your first hour. Go out and walk-run at your target rates. Actively discourage competition. Come back, stretch again and then have your fluids. If it works as it should, a strong pleasant bond will develop among the group members. In fancy terms, this is where the "group process" begins. One way is to get your family involved. There are such families. They all run. Like the Chun family of Honolulu. They call themselves the Hunky Bunch. "Hunky" Chun is a Chinese-American Honolulu physician. He, his wife and their children all run together—it has become their way of life. The Chuns have created a familial group process. The Gookins in San Diego are another example.

Owing to the recent drastic alterations in American familial structure, coupled with the centrifugal mobile aspect of many families, it appears hopeless, or even detrimental in some cases, to attempt to involve family members. Try to extend the concept of the family, your family. Include other people. Running uncles, brothers, sisters, fathers, grandfathers, girl friends, boyfriends, daughters, sons, cousins—it's kind of a fantasy game as these folks get included in your scheme of things. Base the invitation on the desire to run together, the desire to improve physically. Discuss your own weakness— i.e., not having enough of what the cheerleader types call will power—and frankly ask for help. I wouldn't openly mention the idea of an extended family at first. The other person might think you are really nuts and stay away. Keep the focus on the exercise aspects of the whole idea. From the beginning everyone should commit himself to keep moving for the full hour, and the goal should be to jog the full one hour at the target rate. Keep the sessions fun. Talk a lot. Use the simple exercises to keep the legs, shoulders and lower back supple. Discuss diet and vitamins. Argue a bit about what you have read and heard about.

There is another reason for all this talking in these beginning stages. If you are running and are able to talk, you cannot be anaerobic. So, in one way it's a safety valve, a check against someone getting into trouble. Stick together and help each other along.

I now have all six of you, in my mind's eye, three months into the program. You have been wonderfully successful and only occasionally talk about the number of miles you have done. You will have focused on the hour's run, three times a week, with once a week together as a group.

Some of you will have shown the marked addictive aspect and will have started to run on your own. A few of you, maybe all, will have noticed the various altered states of consciousness. Certainly all of you will have increased your sense of well-being and your sense of energy.

Here, after three months, is where some of you may want to attempt to alter other aspects of your life style, whether it is smoking, drinking or eating. But altering life-style patterns isn't easy. There may be a big temptation to take too big a jump. If you find you are not making it—e.g., in dieting—then gently back off on that aspect, but do not stop the running. The time might not be right for you. Keep up the running—for the running is what allows us to have success in these other areas.

I would be a fool to claim or even imply that I knew what was happening inside the human body and brain. All I am saying here is that this simple pattern, applied with consistency, seems to help people to alter self-destructive life-style patterns.

I now see the six of you nine months into the program, and you are running three times a week at your target pulse rates. I have little to say to you any longer. I know I am terribly curious. I want to know what has happened to you. I want to see how many of you will go for the marathon. Have you changed? Do you feel you've changed? I know your heart is better and all that stuff—but did you find something new inside yourself?

If you are curious about your physical changes, you can get a stress test at the end of one year, and you can get all the numbers, Vo_2, etc., you want. If you want to measure yourself psychologically, you could take an MMPI, a Cottrell 16 PF or a Myers-Briggs Test before you start running and the same tests one year later. These tests are all paper-and-pencil stuff, and now the computers can spit out instant results for you to compare in successive years.

Perhaps you'd be satisfied with being able to run a marathon or the memory of a beautiful dawn.

Table I

75% of Maximum Cardiac Output as Pulse Rate
Physically Untrained Adults

Age	Beats	
	One minute	Ten-second target rate
20	148	25
25	146	24
30	144	24
35	143	24
40	142	24
45	140	23
50	138	23
55	137	23
60	135	23
65	134	22
70	132	22
75	131	22
80	129	21
85	128	21

SOURCE: Bruce Protocol

Table II

**75% of Maximum Cardiac Output as Pulse Rate
Physically Trained Adults**

Age	Beats	
	One minute	Ten-second target rate
20	143	24
25	141	24
30	140	23
35	138	23
40	137	23
45	135	23
50	133	22
55	131	22
60	130	22
65	128	21
70	127	21
75	125	21
80	124	21
85	122	20

SOURCE: Bruce Protocol

Table III

How to Take Your Pulse

1. Wear a wristwatch with a sweep-second hand that you can read easily on the dorsum (palm side down) of your left wrist.*
2. Turn the palm of your right hand to the sky.
3. Place the very tips of the fingers of your left hand on your right wrist.
4. Find the bone of your wrist way over to the right, down from the thumb where the wrist and hand join.
5. Move just off the bone to the left, about ⅛ inch, and, pressing firmly with the index, middle and ring fingers, you will feel your pulse.
6. If you can't find it, then go to your jaw with the index finger of your right hand. Find the angle of the jawbone (toward your ear) and go under the bone at that point toward your neck. You should find a strong pulse there.
7. Check your second hand and count your pulse for 10 seconds.

---

* If you wear your watch on your right wrist, reverse the following directions.

Table IV

Outline for Running Life-Style Alteration in Athletically Active* Adults

STEP 1: If over 30, have a physical exam and a stress ECG. If under 30, have just the physical exam.
STEP 2: Run-walk for 1 hour daily at your target rate as determined by your stress test or by Table II.
STEP 3: Add vitamins, yogurt, etc., to your diet as suggested in Chapter 5, Table VII.
STEP 4: Join a marathon clinic and plan to run a marathon.

---

* No high-risk criteria (cf. footnote Table VI) and very active in a sport, e.g., tennis, swimming or cycling, for at least 3 years.

Table V

Outline for Running Life-Style Alteration for Normal* Individuals

STEP 1: If over 30, have a physical exam and a stress ECG—if possible, from a physician who runs. If under 30, have just the physical exam.

STEP 2: For 1 month, run-walk for 1 hour 3 times a week at your target rate as determined by your stress test or by Table I.

STEP 3: Add vitamins, yogurt, etc., to your diet as suggested in Chapter 5, Table VII.

STEP 4: After 1 month, add 1 more day of 1 hour run-walk at target rate, and walk 1 hour a day all other days.

STEP 5: After 2 months at Step 4, run-walk 6 days a week at your target rate. Walk 1 hour the 7th day.

STEP 6: Join a marathon clinic and plan to run a marathon.

---

* No high-risk criteria (cf. footnote Table VI).

Table VI

Outline for Running Life-Style
Alteration for High-Risk Precardiac*

STEP 1: Have a complete physical exam and a stress ECG. You will almost have to find a physician who runs.

STEP 2: For 3 months, run-walk for 1 hour 3 times a week at your target rate as determined by your stress test.

STEP 3: If you feel like it during the first 3 months, walk for 1 hour the other days.

STEP 4: Add vitamins, yogurt, etc., to your diet as suggested in Chapter 5, Table VII.

STEP 5: After 3 months, get a repeat stress ECG and a new target rate.

STEP 6: Add 1 extra hour a week of running.

STEP 7: Keep on the vitamins as in Step 4 and go on a diet. For diets, see Chapter 5, especially Table VIII.

STEP 8: Join a marathon clinic and plan to run a marathon.

---

* High-risk criteria such as obesity, high blood fats, beginning high blood pressure, but no cardiac signs or evidence of any abnormality on ECG.

Use this pattern only if you do not have a medically monitored running program available to you.

5

Metabolic Factors

THE HEART IS COMPOSED OF MUSCLE TISSUE that is different from any other muscle in any part of the body. It is neither smooth nor striated. Under a microscope its distinct appearance makes it specifically identifiable as cardiac muscle. Perhaps the most important thing to understand about the heart is that it is one of the best muscular structures we have in our bodies—no matter what our age, it seems ready to improve its condition if we begin to exercise it in a particular way, a way of running that enables us to reach 75 percent of a predetermined maximum cardiac output—or target rate—for one hour, at least three times a week. With such slow long-distance running certain specific events occur within the heart and blood vessels, and throughout the body. These events are now all well documented and not controversial except to the minds of certain obese, cigarette-smoking, atavistic, sedentary cardiologists.

The first of these changes is in the heart itself. It becomes a better pump; it gets stronger and bigger and does a much better job. For reasons yet unknown, it becomes tremendously less prone to killing itself—and you—via a myocardial infarction if you finish a marathon. This is startling in the face of the fact that we as a nation are in the midst of a cardiac epidemic. It is one of the few tangible bits of information we have to counteract this dreadful killer and crippler. Another thing this running does is increase delivery of oxygen to the muscles of the legs and, since oxygen transport isn't selective in the body, there is at the same time increased delivery of oxygen to all the other parts of the body: the brain, liver, kidneys, skin and genitalia. The heart rate slows down as its ability to pump improves and this, according to many experts, reduces the need for oxygen in the heart itself. The most immediate response is in the muscles that are being used—those in the legs. But as the blood begins to drive through the arteries to meet the demands of the working muscles, various organs are also stimulated. The kidneys are activated to carry off the biochemical waste products of muscular work. The liver begins to fire up its enzyme system to help purify the blood and replace enzymes used in running. At certain points in long-distance running fat cells begin to turn their fats out into the bloodstream so that they can be turned into energy. The lungs, skin, eyes, ears all become involved; the metabolic processes of the entire body are stimulated.

The cardiovascular system reaches into every cell of our body and organ systems, and even the most distant cells respond to the new demands made upon them. The entire body begins to adapt itself to new demands and becomes more efficient, needing less oxygen for the same work load as before and also less lactic-acid production in the muscles. This means there is less fatigue. The best guess is that there are subtle changes in the shape and chemical condition of the muscles themselves to account for this. In my own case my muscles went from chunky in appearance to lean. My forearms used to be thick and blocky. Now they are the forearms of a runner—they look lean. We can only guess why this happens, but we see changes all the time: hidden facial bones appear and the actual contours of the face change. There is a distinct lowering of blood pressure over a period of time (this lowered pressure also reduces the need for oxygen in the heart). There is also a lowering of the blood fats, called the serum triglycerides, which is supposed to be related to the lowering of overall fat content and a help in reducing one's weight. Low blood-sugar levels are raised to normal. Also, abnormal blood sugar responses tend to disappear. I'm not talking about established diabetics. But even with diabetics, this form of running decreases the need for insulin. Combined with a specific diet, some researchers (such as Pritikin) claim to have treated diabetics successfully to the point of not needing to use drugs to adjust the blood-sugar level. All they use is exercise and diet.

An enzyme is a natural catalyst and allows various chemical processes to take place in our bodies. By deliberately creating certain conditions that force the body to go along certain metabolic pathways, we then create further conditions tending to increase the enzymatic and chemical reactions that enable the body to perform a particular task. A good example is the marathon. A marathon is 26 miles, 385 yards. I don't know of anyone who can run that distance without training. And the training is a slow gradual build-up of the body, by slow long-distance running, to be able to run that distance. For example, we now know that if you run an average of 10 miles per day for 90 days prior to a marathon, you will, barring some accident, be able to complete a marathon. As you begin to train for the marathon, your body chemistry alters. You develop the necessary enzymatic and metabolic pathways that will allow you to cover that distance. You will develop a lower heart rate; you will handle the waste products of muscle exercise, such as lactic acid, faster and more efficiently; and you will also begin to "burn" bodily fats instead of sugar. Your body will learn to cool itself off by sweating more freely. And you can assist the whole process by following the suggested diet, vitamins and fasting plans in this book.

Every time you go on a long slow run, all these things are going on inside you. While you are running, enzyme systems are active; the brain is being recharged with new loads of oxygen; old tired glands are reawakened with bursts of fresh oxygenated blood; and if you let all of this happen to you in a regular way, you'll get addicted to an "up" feeling caused by increased physiological activity.

I think it is important to say a few words about metabolism at this point in order to obtain a better understanding of how our bodies work. Let's begin with looking at the common characteristics of all living things. (1) They reproduce themselves. (2) They take in a product (food). And (3) they give off a waste product. This is also true of all aerobic living things, which take in oxygen and give off carbon dioxide as we do, or take in carbon dioxide and give off oxygen, as do plants and anaerobic bacteria. (4) All living things also give off heat. They may be frozen solid at times, but when they return to life, they again produce heat. Thus, the characteristics of life common to all living things are really simple: trees, turtles, apes, bacteria and men all do the same things.

Now we all know that to be true—or do we? Let's return to metabolism. It's not a mysterious process at all. It is simply the way our cells burn fuel. In some senses it is better to think of metabolism as controlled burning. When we eat, our food turns to fuel, which we "burn" or metabolize. If we fast, our body must use fuel we have stored in our fat cells in order to obtain enough energy to keep going. If we fast too long, the process will turn on our muscles themselves. So, in a way, we are on fire, and we can consume ourselves, which is called starving to death.

When we have a serious bacterial illness, our entire

metabolic rate increases and we have a fever. This is another way to die from this burning process—by getting too hot. Let our fever get too high too long, and sensitive cells die off and we die from the fever. However, some marathon runners develop a core body temperature—that is, inside the body rather than under the tongue—as high as 106° F. This comes from the "work" or metabolism of the muscles and the cardiovascular system, plus a wide host of enzymes and hormones that are stimulated by the running process. For example, growth stimulating hormones are released from the pituitary after forty minutes or so of running at 75 percent of maximum cardiac output.

What makes it possible for the Tarahumara Indians to run races 150 miles in length over rough mountainous terrain? Do we believe the reports of the Tibetan monks who in a trance state can run for 24 hours without stopping at a pace of 7 minutes per mile? And these same monks have apparently had to learn to control their metabolic processes so that they can sit out in freezing weather all night and have water poured over themselves.

Somewhere in all of this is a clue to an unknown frontier. Is this a learned process? Is it possible for us to "learn" to control our metabolic processes? For even in this arena of "learning" and "memory" we have data that confounds us. If cats are taught to run a maze and then their forebrains are removed, they are then unable to run the maze. If, however, they are overtrained to run the maze and then their forebrains are removed, they can then run the maze with ease. The learning was "transferred to a lower center." When we do lobotomies on people we call patients, they do not forget their language. It has been "overtrained" or "overlearned."

I think that it is possible to retrain and then overtrain metabolic processes. But this has to be accomplished in an indirect manner. For example, I cannot sit still and through some process of meditation stimulate the enzyme systems to increase their activity in order to dispose of excess lactic acid. However, I can run slow long distances on a regular basis and, with the constant repetition, those enzymes will be stimulated.

Even changes in sexual responses have been linked to running. It is difficult to arrive at any clear picture in this area, as we are engaged in making major changes in our sexual behavior in the United States. Many people are interested in "quantity"—especially men. And according to the men who will discuss this with me, they all agree that the quantity is increased by running. In fact, the other day while I was speaking to the San Diego Surgical Society, a urologist in the audience reported that he personally knew of two cases of impotence cured by slow long-distance running. That seemed to be a nice result, and I'm certain the men who had the experience appreciated what had happened to them. Since most cases of impotence are psychogenic in origin, maybe that enriched flow of oxygen to the brain is what changed things around.

As a male, in the current politically sexual context, I hesitate to make any comments on the changes in women who run. I can only give my subjective response, and that is that they look beautiful. Their grace and form, the increased clarity of their skin and a whole host of other factors that are best placed in the aesthetic realm seem to blossom. I have watched ungainly, stumbling girls slowly change to lithe, graceful, even beautiful women. There is something especially sensuous about a woman running. It is the sensuousness of a fresh clear breeze from the sea, not the smoke-filled stench of the bar. The running woman seems to show a special strength and poise and to know that she is beautiful. And I think this concept of the aesthetics of beauty begins to change the usual notions of sexuality in men from the importance of quantity to an increased appreciation of quality. I don't know how to measure all this; all I know is its pleasure.

There is so much interest today in diets and dieting, vitamins, nutrition and all the rest that we are probably on the threshold of a whole new era of dietary management and therapy. Certain things which seem quite true today may change tomorrow, but some facts will remain. One is that no one will be able to lose much weight just by running—unless, of course, he keeps his caloric intake set at the same level as before running. Most people automatically adjust and begin to increase their caloric intake, and their weight stays the same.

In any case, it is better not to change your diet in the first three months; leave it alone. Eat and drink what you like. Concentrate on establishing your pattern of running one hour, three times a week. However, over a later period of time I lost a lot of weight, and so have many other runners. I'd like to offer a regime that can help you with both running and losing weight, when you are ready. (See Table VII.)

Injuries, fatigue and illness often occur when people fail to take the one gram of vitamin C for every 6 miles they run. The brewer's yeast, yogurt and wheat-germ oil all seem to be helpful, and I have observed that the runners who do not continue to add these to their diet get into difficulty, having problems with their leg muscles and tendons. Their legs ache too much and they appear to be prone to torn muscles or ligaments, as happened to me. The later addition of foods and the vitamins to the diet appears to promote skin changes—the runner looks younger and fresher.

The basic rules are always to keep at the minimum of three hours a week, watch the vitamins and slow down. Let your body change slowly. Discover your internal signals that can help you to avoid becoming a running dropout. Some of these internal signals may appear odd to you, but I suggest you follow them. For example,

Table VII

Dietary Principles for Runners

1. Eat only when you are hungry.
2. Eat less than you think you need.
3. Drink a lot of water. If you are thirsty, it's too late—drink water when you are not thirsty.
4. Take any suitable multivitamin every day.
5. Take 1 gram (1000 mg.) of vitamin C for each hour of running. Vitamin C seems to protect the muscles and ligaments against injury. Don't take more than that, though. Too much is just wasted.
6. Take 4 tablespoons of brewer's yeast powder in water or juice every morning. This is a marvelous, inexpensive source of B vitamins.
7. Eat a cup of nonfat, plain yogurt each day (no sugar-containing fruit types). Yogurt also helps the gut supply B vitamins by assisting and stabilizing in the intestines the bacteria that make B vitamins.
8. Take 1 tablespoon of wheat-germ oil twice a day. This provides vitamin E and unsaturated fatty acids, both of which are said to help metabolize other fats in the body.
9. Make certain you take in enough potassium via the foods you eat.
10. Eat ½ cup of coarse bran daily.
11. Stay away from processed, prepared foods if at all possible.
12. Read the labels on everything you eat and avoid strange-sounding or -looking chemicals.
13. Avoid saturated fats.
14. Avoid sugar (sucrose).
15. Avoid all tobacco and use coffee and alcohol sparingly if at all.

a common problem is an aching lower back. Try then to work on various ways to stretch your lower back. Try some yoga. Do sit-ups with your arms folded over your chest and knees bent. Change your mattress. Try sleeping on the floor. Work at your lower back; find out what works for you. Naps are also important. If at all possible, try a brief nap whenever you can.

When I return home from a morning run, I kick my shoes off and step into the shower with all my running clothes on. They stink anyway and need to be washed. I stretch my lower back in the shower and slowly strip. I hang the sloppy clothes on the faucet and let them drip out there. Later, on the way back through the bathroom, I dump them directly into the washing machine. When I'm out of the shower, I try to avoid any chilling and then lie down for five to ten minutes and just rest. If before running you are excessively fatigued, go out for your hour, but allow yourself the option of walking for that hour. It may be what your body needs. Try it and see. You may find it's okay to jog a bit, and the fatigue may go away. Don't chain yourself to a scheme, such as a graph of miles and numbers. Use the scheme as a guide; don't be rigid about it. If you fall short, don't just chuck the whole thing. Maybe you were not supposed to run that day and you needed the rest.

If you get a cold, don't get hysterical about it, either by going to bed in fear of rampant pneumonia or by getting up and running 30 miles in the snow wearing only your shorts and shoes. Enter into your cold gingerly. Go out for your run, but dress quite warmly. Before the run take two aspirin with a little milk. Then see if you feel okay while running. If you do, be certain to keep checking your pulse rate; then go ahead and run. But be certain to stay warm, almost hot. Come home and fix yourself a big cup of hot coffee or tea. Add honey if you wish and take some salt, either on celery or straight or any way you want. Then draw a really hot bath, get in and boil away, and then go to bed for a few hours. When you wake up, your cold may very well be gone. If it isn't, it usually means you're in for a siege and it's time to let the cold have its day. Try to weather the cold with the notion that it's building antibodies for you so you won't get the next one.

Some people develop a chronic electrolyte depletion over a period of time. An excellent electrolyte replacement fluid for runners in ERG. It's made here in San Diego by Bill Gookin and we call it Gookinade. I like it and use it. Other people find and swear by their own concoctions. For example, tomato juice is an excellent electrolyte replacement fluid as long as you drink an equal amount of water. Broths and bouillons are also good. A fun-tasting drink can be made with one quart of Tang, one quart of apple juice and one pint of cranberry juice, mixed all together and served very cold. The trouble with this particular drink is that it has sucrose in it.

After the first three months you should begin to notice the development of new tastes and appetites, or loss of interest in certain foods. Follow these interests. See where they take you. If you are interested in losing weight and are the kind of person who is able to sustain a diet, find one you like and go on a diet that is 1,500 calories per day. Keep up the suggestions in Table VII as well. On 1,500 calories a day, along with the multivitamins, vitamin C, brewer's yeast, and water, you should begin to lose weight. The biggest problem with people who diet and lose weight is that they just go right back up again after a couple of months. However, there are people who are successful in their change of body weight over a long period. They begin to notice how they function best. They change slowly as they experiment with themselves. This is one reason why there are so many different diets. Each one seems to work for some portion of the population.

The people who have the hardest time are those who become chronically obese. I was one of these people.

Studies of very obese people indicate that they have lost the ability to recognize both hunger and satiety. They refer to external, not internal cues as to whether they eat or not. Thus, they respond to taste, the time of the day and the social aspects. They don't seem to know when they are hungry or not. With some people, the best way to lose weight while keeping up their running is to fast. It is usually easier on them, because they do not experience hunger and they are better able to control their appetites and volume. I therefore offer this type of plan for those of you who want to take off the weight you don't want. This is the technique that helped me lose weight.

First of all, remember to keep up the running and try this pattern only after the first three months. Keep up the multivitamins, vitamin C, brewer's yeast and especially the increased intake of water. Eat your Sunday evening dinner and then do not eat anything until Tuesday breakfast. Eat lightly and avoid the usual fattening foods on Tuesday and Wednesday. Then, after dinner Wednesday, fast again until Friday morning breakfast. Here you have two periods a week of fasting. Your stomach will contract in size, and if you begin to make a continued habit of this pattern of fasting, you will lose weight. Be certain you don't get the "rebound idea" and pig it up on the days you have not fasted. That will only mess up the works and you won't lose any weight. The only thing you should ingest on the fasting days is water. Avoid all other foods and liquids, especially coffee, tea and noncaloric soft drinks. Again, gently experiment with yourself and watch the results. The key is the running, the basic running pattern as habit, which will help you in your attempts to change. One man at the marathon clinic found he lost 40 pounds easily by drinking a gallon of apple cider every two days and avoiding eating heavily in the evening. Some Eastern monastic groups avoid food after noon, but eat all they wish between sunrise and noon. They all seem to stay thin. Others have found that yogurt and fresh fruit every day aid their weight-losing process.

Another approach is the carbohydrate-loading diet that many marathon runners use. It begins six days before the marathon. You start out by running 20 miles and then the diet begins. For the first three days there is an absolute prohibition against carbohydrates. Fish, meat and cheese, water, vitamin C, other vitamins and wheat-germ oil are okay. The runner runs at a low rate for one hour the second day and on the third day he runs for an hour and then goes off the no-carbohydrate, protein-rich part of the program. In these first three days you usually feel rotten. Halitosis is extreme and you must watch out for infections. Keep drinking plenty of water. Then after that run on the third day, start taking in carbohydrates. Eat natural carbohydrates such as rice, potatoes, fruits and milk. Avoid sugars. On the fifth day eat very sparingly, and don't eat any solids for twelve to fifteen hours before the marathon. Many marathoners have a spaghetti dinner as their last meal before the marathon. The theory behind this is that the muscle fibers get depleted of glycogen in the first three days and then rebound and more or less stuff themselves in the next two days so that they are primed to perform a good marathon. This diet does not produce any weight loss.

Another diet for long-distance runners is the seven-day one shown in Table VIII.

Whatever you do—diet, pace, dress, time of running—think of yourself as an experiment of one. Recognize that you are unique. Experiment gently. What may work for one person may be detrimental to another. And don't hurry the process. Continue the basic running pattern and watch your own responses. Your body may respond slowly, but if you keep at it, you will find the pattern that best fits you. You will know you have found it when it works for you. Be careful of overdoing it—it is possible to run too much. When you run 100 miles a week or more, you are inviting injury. You will either come down with a physical illness—something like the flu—or with a torn, sprained or severely strained muscle or ligament.

One of the problems we have in our culture is the one called competition. We can compete with others or with ourselves. The people who run marathons and begin to drive themselves harder and harder against their own time factors, or who compete against another person in a serious way, often develop a haggard and rather nonmellow way of looking at running. It becomes another task, a chore, and they develop injuries and eventually drop out. I know this from my own experience in the fall of 1974. I was training for the Seattle Marathon, which was to be run on November 30. I wanted to break 3½ hours and I set up a daily hard pace. I ran two hours a day. Often I ran from 4 A.M. to 6 A.M. At that rate, I was covering about 100 miles a week. I neglected my vitamin intake, didn't pay attention to my increasing fatigue and, at the end of the second week of this high training, partially avulsed (tore) my right Achilles tendon. Fortunately it healed—but I could have done some severe damage.

The Seattle Marathon experience also alerted me to the effects and problems associated with temperature, altitude and humidity. When we run, we generate heat. This heat is lost through sweating, which, when it evaporates, cools the body. We also lost some heat via our lungs as we breathe in dry air and breathe out moist, warmed air. If the temperature goes up too high or the humidity is too high or both, we can get into trouble. Our body temperature rises when we cannot rid ourselves of the unwanted heat. So the best bet is to slow down and drink a lot of fluid. The symptoms to watch for are dizziness, a throbbing heart and dry skin. If you feel any of these, stop and cool down. The increase of body temperature in runners has been measured and can go as high as 106° F. in a marathon. With a core body temperature that high, the runner is on the edge of disaster. There are two specific syndromes that can oc-

Table VIII

Long-Distance Runner's Seven-Day
Weight-Loss Diet*

1. Run 1 hour each day.
2. Drink at least 4 quarts of water each day.
3. Continue the vitamins as suggested in Table VII, items 4, 5 and 8, plus the brewer's yeast, item 6, in some of the liquids listed below.

Monday:	6 hard-boiled eggs
	1 quart of orange juice
Tuesday:	1 quart of whole milk
	1 quart of apple juice
Wednesday:	200 grams of rice
	1 quart of orange juice
Thursday:	1 pint of yogurt
	1 quart of apple juice
Friday:	1 quart of orange juice
	1 quart of whole milk
	4 pieces of rye toast
Saturday:	1 quart of apple juice
	4 pieces of wheat toast
Sunday:	½ broiled chicken
	1 quart of beer

Note: If you get weak during this diet, use a herb tea with honey.

---

* To use this diet properly, you must already have run several marathons and be in excellent physical condition. If you have any doubts, consult your physician.

cur. The first is heat exhaustion. In this situation the runner's skin is wet. He is fatigued and may be dizzy. A persistent headache is a dangerous symptom. The treatment for heat exhaustion is rest and fluids. The runner may ignore the symptoms of heat exhaustion and continue to drive himself. Then heat stroke may occur. The symptoms are headache, a chilly sensation, goose bumps, disorientation and dry skin. At this point the sweat reflex has stopped and the body temperature is soaring. This now becomes a medical emergency. The runner should be stopped and cooled off as soon as possible and taken to a hospital. But heat exhaustion and heat stroke can be avoided by taking in a lot of fluid, not driving yourself and keeping cool. Often on a long run, especially if it's warm, we will pour water over ourselves. Again it's a matter of personal experience. I have taken a garden hose and drenched myself during a marathon and delighted in the feeling. I cooled off and it was delicious. But I know other runners who avoid the cold water on their body and only cool their face and head. Dr. Jack Scaff, who lives in Honolulu and runs there, always wears a navy-blue knit watch cap. In the heat of Honolulu I always wondered about it until he told me that during a long run he puts crushed ice under his cap. It cools his scalp, and the cap holds the ice in place.

There are probably specific benefits of the rise in body temperature that we do not yet fully understand. The rise in temperature will be accompanied by a generalized increase in metabolic activity throughout the body. The success of the runner's remedy for the common cold may have something to do with the induction of a low-grade fever while running. It is an area that has not received much attention, but I feel that the increase in body temperature while the body is working may have a lot to do with the clearing and removal of waste products and the stimulation of the endocrine system, and it may even have a direct effect on the metabolism of the brain.

Another hazard is the sun. I have to watch my nose and cheeks to prevent them from getting too burned. A sun-screen lotion is good. Another useful item is a visor that helps shade your face. While on the topic of heat and clothing, light-reflecting colors are cooler. A simple white cotton T-shirt is an excellent piece of clothing. It reflects heat, is highly visible and holds the sweat so that it can perform its cooling function. Sweat that drips off is a loss to you.

I knew all this about heat, and I had read about the chill factor of running when it's very cold outside. In those places like Alaska, or maybe Boston and Chicago, where it can get pretty cold in the winter, the runner has to protect himself with enough clothing to prevent frostbite and extreme heat loss. Jackets, sweaters, pants, caps and socks are in order, and the runner must dress for the weather. But, here I was, training—and in some respects overtraining—for the Seattle Marathon.

I started out that marathon with cap and jacket on over my tank top and shorts. It was a cool day, but as I warmed up, I took off the jacket and the cap. I felt just fine and warm enough at the 5-and 10-mile marks. But my desire to beat 3½ hours robbed me of my ability to think of the weather and its effect on me. The drug of competition had blinded me to myself. I wasn't used to running in temperatures between 30° and 40° F., and I think my core body temperature began to drop at about the 16-mile mark. I first noticed a severe cramp in the muscles of my right leg, up in the hamstrings. The cramping soon spread to both legs. I was miserable. My arms and face were numb from the cold, but I didn't seem to realize that I could get too cold and I didn't ask for a cap or jacket from my wife as she met me at various points on the course. I think my body responded to the cold by shutting down its peripheral blood supply to conserve heat, which meant less blood to my leg muscles. At any rate, the pain was horrible and I ran slower and slower. I knew that I was very close to making it at 3½ hours in the last 5 miles, but the pain, cramping and fatigue made it impossible for me to go any faster. For those last 5 miles I was in such terrible pain that I was crying. I was in the grip of this competitive demon, pushing myself. When I crossed the finish line, my time was 3 hours, 31 minutes and 17 seconds. I had missed the 3½ hour mark by 1 minute, 17 seconds. I couldn't walk afterward and I was miserable. I had made myself miserable by pushing too hard and not taking care of myself. I experienced a severe depression for one week after that marathon.

In training people it becomes very hard to teach them to slow their pace. A very simple but surprisingly effective remedy for an aching knee, foot or ankle is to continue to run but to run slower and slower until the ache or pain disappears. Try not to compete, even with yourself. Especially don't do so in your daily runs. Go slowly.

The basic, minimal formula is three hours a week at 75 percent of your maximum cardiac output. If you have advanced your cardiovascular status to the point where you have already finished a marathon, try to make your running more enjoyable, not more competitive. Find your pride in your personal growth, not in comparison—in the joy of running.

6

Psychological Effects

THE OTHER DAY A VERY ARTICULATE MAN of forty-nine invoked the privilege of confidentiality with me. He wanted to tell me something but made me promise not to tell who he was. He said he had been running for ten years, since he was thirty-nine. He has lost about 50 pounds, has stopped smoking and does his run every morning. He runs before dawn, or just about dawn, depending on the time of year. He doesn't talk to anyone about his running—and it was only after talking to me about these "discoveries" that he decided to tell me his story. He said that his life is full of stress and competition every day. In his job, daily, he has to meet competition and there isn't any place he is able to find solace or reflection. He knows that his creativity is somehow tied with his running.

When I encouraged him to run with the San Diego Marathon Clinic or to run a marathon, he pulled back as if he had seen a rattlesnake. He said: "If I did that, I'd be around other people. I wouldn't have the experiences that I get every day, just about, and I know that I would become competitive. That competition would destroy it all for me. I've got to stay away from that sort of thing." And then he began to describe what happened to him on his daily 10-mile runs. His major ecstasy was the smells he encountered. He told me with the greatest delight about one morning when he could smell the odors from a restaurant he knew was at least 3 miles away. He runs in an area where the early morning winds blow very lightly and can come from almost any direction—including the ocean, which is only a half mile away.

I can see him secretly dressing for his early morning run. Putting on his running stuff, an early morning ritual. A devoted monk anticipating his first Mass of the day. The air is cold. He enters a world that is silent and full of things that are mysterious in the half light of the dying night and the coming day. It is as if he himself has turned back along the revolutionary trail fifty thousand, a hundred thousand years. He becomes ancient man again. The hunter. Out early, his senses alert, his blood powerfully flowing as he jogs along. Soon the pores of his skin open: he sweats. His eyes clear. His nerves, all of them, become alert. And the most primitive sense organ of man, the sense of smell, is triggered.

One hundred thousand years ago, a small, small time in biological history, man did not have to compete with man. There were few men—but many animals. Man the running animal could run alone, scenting, looking, scouting, warming up. Other men were of his clan or small group. Sharing and warmth were known, not hostility, overcrowding, competition and war. It is similar to the Eskimo way of life as they were, before we had influenced them. There are forces enough in nature to deal with, both visible and invisible, to take all our energies. Another man is a brother, not someone to be feared.

My secret runner also described his sense of well-being and feeling refreshed after a run. He also talked about that feeling of being able to run as if he were a little bit off the ground—about a foot or so—and a sense of brightness and delight that came near the end of his 45- to 60-minute run. I stopped my missionary push and respected his confidence. I suspect that there are more men who have found this for themselves.

The various mental, emotional or psychic phenomena of running can be divided into various categories. Perhaps it's best to divide them into what one can expect to experience on a typical run of one hour.

Now the conditions of the run are critical ingredients in how one obtains these effects. In a race or in any form of competition, the runner does not usually experience them. We are so trained to be competitive that we tend to carry that competition right along with us, such as, "Well, I made that three miles in thirty minutes yesterday; I'll do it in twenty-seven minutes today." That kind of attitude is destructive in relation to these phenomena. It orients the runner away from himself; it focuses his mind on an artificial target or graph. It pins him to a chart and makes him a number or statistic. It's like going to prison, losing your name and getting a number instead. Mental uplift will not be noticed if you run with others unless you know the people you run with very well. It will also seldom occur if you run in an area that is unfamiliar to you, for the strangeness of the surroundings will take your attention away from yourself.

Now with all those warnings, which aren't many, let's see what happens in the run. And again, by run I mean 75 percent of your maximum cardiac output, which to almost everyone is a slow, easy jog, during which, if you have to, you are able to carry on a conversation with ease.

The first twenty minutes. In most cases people feel stiff or slow. I often feel rotten and wonder why in the hell I'm doing this. It seems hard to get the system going. (Sometimes, however, there is an exuberance.) Dysphoria most often occurs in this first twenty minutes. That word "dysphoria," if you sound it out, tells its own story. It means feeling bad. A nasty, no-good, sour-taste-in-the-mouth mood. Don't be alarmed if this happens. Check your watch and pulse and keep on going.

Twenty to 30 minutes. Here the dysphoria will, if it is happening, peak. This is the point where some people begin to cry. They may feel it coming on earlier, but the actual tears erupt at this time—and sometimes continue. It's as if this upwelling of tears is necessary for the person. It may not be depression at all. Those who have told me about it say it actually feels good, or right, to cry, but they want to be away from other people because others, they feel, won't understand why they are crying. Almost everyone would want them to stop running or be sympathetic. Naturally, this is not at all what they want at that time. The first hump is the 30-minute mark. But remember, if you continue to feel bad after 30 minutes of running, then I'd advise you to stop. It usually means something is wrong. Most often I've found that it means the onset of a cold, or you need to adjust your diet or vitamins or you have been training too hard. One of the problems we Americans have is that we are quite often—too often—out of touch with and unaware of our bodily feelings. We lack a sense of our body. We do not "listen" to it.

I have heard of three men who died while running. Two of them were joggers who had severe heart disease. Their physicians warned them to stay within specific limits and to avoid experiencing any angina or chest pain. Both ran hard, experienced the chest pain, ignored it and died. The third man had decided to run, but did not get a physical examination or stress test. He was in his mid-fifties and an aggressive, hard-driving, successful businessman. He experienced severe chest pain on a Saturday night with cold sweating. He ignored the pain. On Sunday morning he turned out for a meeting of a marathon clinic and did not listen to the warning given to all beginners. He ran hard, jaw tight, hands like fists, and he dropped dead. An autopsy showed that he had had a coronary the night before he died.

So please, listen to your body and follow what it tells you.

Between 30 and 40 minutes some people experience the "opening up" phenomenon. They begin to breathe more freely, their chest lifts and the entire system seems to work more at ease. It's a powerful, wonderful feeling. It's akin to waking something up inside you. You've got to pay attention to yourself to find it, and a lot of things can distract you, such as competition, cars, dogs, people. As I'll say over and over, just about any of the phenomena of running can be shut off by external distractions. This is an area where I have a bit of conflict with the point system in aerobics. The focus of this new technique on the points puts one's attention outside. In this situation it can be dangerous. For example, in *The New Aerobics*, on page 29, Dr. Cooper describes the twelve-minute test: "Run and walk as far as you comfortably can in twelve minutes. If you get winded, slow down awhile until you get your breath back. Then run again for a stretch. The idea is to cover the greatest distance you can in those twelve minutes." Here I see the invitation to disaster. It is a competition. It is *against* those twelve minutes. And we Americans have a crazy quirk about us. We respond to external challenge as a highly bred Spanish bull responds to the flapping cape. Directed properly, this drive can help us accomplish tremendous feats of humanitarian service, scientific endeavor and other good things. However, I think it's only how we develop personalities that lead to early death from coronary disease. Our aggressive drive is a force, neither good nor evil, and we can channel it toward these quiet nice discoveries of what lives within ourselves. Turn to your pulse—your own pulse rate as the direct connection with your heart— and hope that it turns your attention inward. Especially now, 30 to 45 minutes into the run, for just at this time, the first of the possible alterations in consciousness begins to occur. These alterations are usually sensory. The senses seem to increase in alertness. All of them respond: sight, hearing, touch, taste, smell and position. You may be lucky to get one of those especially vivid moments that become your private personal treasures for the rest of your life. I'd like to share two of them with you. The first one was visual and, in fact, was the experience that led me to look into this whole thing.

I was running on the beach at Torrey Pines in the afternoon. I had been running for 45 minutes. I looked up and saw a seagull. It's absurd, isn't it? A seagull in San Diego, where there are so many of them. But what happened was a moment of aesthetic arrest. I didn't "see" that seagull. I had a glad, flying, delightful, deep inner penetration of my mind and soul that was triggered off by that seagull. I was astonished. It was all the grace of its flying, all the dreams of air and freedom and beauty of all the seagulls I've ever seen rolled into one tightly compacted vision. The experience is still with me. I had found something beautiful within myself. I have had considerable difficulty in describing this phenomenon, as it does not exactly accord with any of the other altered states of consciousness of current interest such as occur in meditation, drugs, biofeedback and so on. It is clearly peculiar to running and specifically occurs only after 40 minutes of running.

Another experience occurred when I was in Honolulu in December, 1974, speaking and waiting to run the Honolulu Marathon. I got up quite early one morning and ran toward Diamond Head on a training run. I went up and it was dark. Dawn was yet to come. I turned around after going a half hour and started down. I felt good, relaxed and easy. There were very few people around. Suddenly, ahead of me was a tiny blond girl, with long straight hair, pushing her bike. It had a load of undelivered newspapers on the front handlebars in one of those gray bags. As I closed the gap, she seemed to be limping. As I went past, I said, "Hi, something wrong with your leg?" She said, "No, it's my chain and my pants." Although it had been thirty years since it had happened to me, I knew what she meant. Her pants fabric was caught between the chain and sprockets. I turned around and mumbled something like "Let me help," and she hesitated, not wanting to bother me, but I just went ahead and pushed the pedal forward and her trousers came free. All in all this whole business lasted about ten seconds. And then, in the dim morning light, she looked up at me and smiled and said, "Thanks." She was about six or seven. And it happened again. That smile penetrated into the murky depths of my memory and released all the loves, pleasures, kindnesses, tendernesses of all the women I have ever known. There was also in that little girl the interlocking of Helen of Troy, Mary, Eve and Aphrodite, and these, too, were brought to my conscious attention. By this time I knew about this phenomenon and was delighted as I finished the run back to the hotel. Was I, as a buddy of mine said, just a dirty old man? Well, I wouldn't totally deny his interpretation, but it once again had the *quality* of the seagull experience. I looked at my watch, and again it was in the 45-minute range.

There are certain characteristics of this phenomenon. You will know it by the quality of its appearance. I've never found it in anyone except after 40 minutes of this kind of running. It isn't always a "peak" experience. One time it was the beauty of the red color of a fireplug. Just the red color, that red color, nothing more. But that red color, that time, was the nicest, neatest, brightest, finest red in the world. I could almost taste it. It happens suddenly. It's as if a trapdoor had sprung open into some secret treasure trove hiding within us.

Finding out about this feeling from others is a difficult task. Most of us hesitate to tell anyone about it for fear the other person will think we are a bit crazy. However, with people who understand this and aren't afraid to talk about it, I've heard some really wonderful stories. "It happened with my legs. They didn't want to stop running. They were just having fun going and going." Another man to whom I had talked about this was all excited when he told me, "It happened! Finally the grass looked like it was a fluorescent green!"

I'd like to quote Sir Arthur Eddington's *Nature of the Physical World*: "We have torn away the mental forces to get at the reality beneath, only to find that the reality of that which is beneath is bound up with the potentiality of awakening these forces. It is because the mind, the weaver of illusion, is also the only guarantor of reality that reality is always to be sought at the base of illusion."

There are four categories of the phenomenon which I have found to occur in the period after 40 minutes. They are sensory, emotional, a category I'll call clearing the field, and the fourth I call the K phenomenon, which I have just described. As in any function of the mind, it is impossible to separate the categories such as memory fully from thinking or emotion. I have briefly touched on the sensory experiences, which apparently are related to, or trigger, the K phenomenon. There are other sensory phenomena, but all seem, as mentioned above, to be related to increased sensation. In the area of the emotional changes I have mentioned the appearance of depression prior to the 30-minute period of time. One very interesting piece of observation is that ordinary garden varieties of depression disappear after 40 minutes.

The most commonly experienced emotion is a mild euphoria, or "runner's high." This high is very specific when it occurs and is probably related to different personality types. People who like to get high return over and over again for the experience.

The other day, Nancy, a member of the first

research group at San Diego State, told me that at around 40 minutes she felt she had to cry. She said she wasn't depressed at all. It was, she said, a kind of necessary upwelling and the only thing she was worried about was the concern of the other group members. She said she liked it. One of the male members of that same group, Ozzie, reported the same sensation without the appearance of the tears. He seemed to think that it benefited him as well.

Anger is usually considered an emotion. The feeling I've discovered here is that the individual is usually not able to hold onto intense anger after 30 minutes (however, I've also heard runners talk about anger directed against cars and nasty dogs). I think the only time anger really begins to dominate the scene is when the running is competitive. I know one runner who has a perpetual anger directed against automobiles. He's a big man, 6 feet 6 inches tall and fairly muscular. One day a car passed him and two guys made some nasty crack at him as they drove by. At the next intersection they were stopped by a red light. He was so delighted to see them that he ran over the car stomping on its trunk, roof and hood.

"Clearing the field" is perhaps a clumsy term, but it's the best one I knew. I'll try to describe it. Prior to the run I may have a particular and specific problem with which I am wrestling. I can recall a specific example. I wanted to clarify the explicit differences between Freudian and Jungian analytic practices. I had been struggling with the question for a couple of days. I went for a run, still thinking about it. At around 30 minutes I found I couldn't hold onto the problem any longer. At around 35 to 40 minutes, the issue became distasteful. I had, then, a series of disjointed, odd facts, notions and bits and pieces of flotsam and jetsam seemingly not at all related to the problem I was working on. Finally, after I returned home and as I cooled down, I refocused my attention on the original problem, and there lay, in my mind's eye, a clear, logical and concise contrast between the two forms of analysis. It was as if I had "consulted" another portion of my mind. This consultant responded first by clearing my conscious mind of the problem and throwing in the proper amount of other material to help arrange the synthesis. In speaking to runners I have found many who have experienced the same thing with only minor variations. Some author-runners make the statement that their personal creativity is directly connected to their running.

I'm sure that these experiences are closely related to meditation. The clearing of consciousness, the ability to find a central focus within, the delight of a clear mind, the sense of refreshment of the soul are reported both by those who practice meditation and by long-distance runners. The difference between the two techniques is in the physical effects of the running. It is as if those who meditate have found one half the picture. The runners who just compete and do not reach for the psychological aspects have found the other half. The runners who are able to slow down and search for the psychic aspects will have both—the soul and the body.

I also feel that there is a distinct religious dimension, which must be mentioned. I know several people who have connected their experiences of slow long-distance running with prayer and religious insight. They have found a sense of being closer to God and to others while running.

By now, your mind should be buzzing with associations like meditation, religious experience, psychedelics, right side of the brain, collective unconscious, transcendence, peak experience, alpha waves and so on. I like the concept of Western Zen. For the Zen part the experiences are clear once you've had them. The Western part is that there is a nice formula to achieve these things. And that is, walk, run, jog at 75 percent of your maximum cardiac output, for one hour, a minimum of three times a week. Don't compete; run easily; turn your attention inward toward yourself.

111

Naturally, I've got a theory about all this, but I'll try to put it in a place where you can read it, if interested. That's the next chapter, "Theory." Maybe, however, you may have a better theory than mine. If it works for you, that's all that really counts.

7

Theory

IN ONE SENSE THIS CHAPTER isn't really necessary: I hope you will evolve your own theory or theories about what takes place within you as you run. However, I found it necessary to attempt to explain, for myself, why these things seem to happen. Why do these changes take place? I hope this "theory" will act as a challenge and a stimulus to you. And I hope that people will try to disprove it. At least then they will be interested and work on the many issues raised for ourselves and our culture.

So many physical changes result from exercise that there is a mountain of literature about them. But there is very little about the psychological aspects, and there is very little in the literature at all in the way of a comprehensive theory that approaches this form of running from the perspective of the development of man as a species.

One research group ran mice on a treadmill over a prolonged period of time. They found that there was a 20 percent increase in blood flow to the brain. It is clear, from indirect studies in man (the mouse research was direct—they killed the animals to obtain the results) that a similar process occurs. There is a marked increase in blood flow to the brain. In my opinion, after going over the literature on this subject, the increase is at least 20 percent, if not more. Now it would seem that the brain would be the last place for blood to flow when we are running. The need is in the muscles of the legs and in the heart itself. What use is all that blood up there inside the skull? One of the answers is that we lose a lot of heat from our heads. In running a marathon, for instance, one of the things that has been measured is a core body temperature of 106° F. One of the best ways to cool off is to pour water over one's head. Sweating helps, too. However, we know that certain centers in the brain are directly related to running. The first of these is the cortical motor strip. That is the center of all voluntary motor activity. But with rhythmic slow running, lower centers in the brain apparently begin to take over. We stop "thinking" about it. It seems as if we could run forever. We suddenly feel free and easy. Now one of the strange aspects of the voluntary motor cortex is that highly conscious motor activity requires what feels subjectively like hard work. We have to concentrate on it. But if we do it long enough, it becomes automatic; it seems to be transferred to another area of our brain that is less conscious. This phenomenon occurs in studying, in which we cease to learn well after about 30 minutes and should take a break to let the conscious part of our mind take a rest. In learning a foreign language, the same thing seems to happen. It is difficult in its initial stages; then later it becomes automatic. At first it is a struggle. Then as we progress it becomes less difficult, and finally we can "think" in the new language. In children this process is faster. A child's brain seems more plastic than that of an adult.

To translate this brain phenomenon into the process of slow long-distance running, I liken the running itself to one of the major techniques of meditation, and sometimes prayer, employed by virtually all disciplines both East and West: the constant repetition of a particular word or series of words, whether it be, "Om, na pad na, om na" or the Hail Mary. It matters little what value that particular philosophy or religion attaches to the use of the word, phrase or prayer. It is clearly intended to be an opening into another aspect of awareness. In short, by means of the repetition, the phenomenon sought—namely, the touching of another state of consciousness—is achieved. I think the same process occurs in the repetitive rhythm of slow long-distance running. Eventually, at somewhere between thirty and forty minutes, the conscious mind gets exhausted and other areas of consciousness are activated.

Now at this point I should like to explain further my position regarding this phenomenon. It has become a habit for me, as a physician and scientist, to attempt to answer virtually every question by reducing it to the proposition "Is it this or that?" In this situation, such a black-and-white approach seems to do violence to what I perceive to be at least a rainbow of effects. Black and white are included, but so are a host of other colors. Thus, it becomes "this and that and that and that. . . ." One of the first "thats" to occur, I think, is the exhaustion of the left side of the cerebral cortex. This is the dominant, logical, sequentially ordered side of our brain. The use of logic can lead to sterility and cynicism. Consistency and logic teamed together in our time often seem to produce results that, with any examination at all, lead to absurdity. We hold fast to certain patterns long after their usefulness is worn out. We have been told and trained that logic is our best friend, our aid and ally. But we have not been trained to see that it is only one of our tools, and that there are others that can help us. The repetitive running mode, just like the repetitive "Om," wears out the left cortex and allows consciousness to take a peek at the functions of the right side of the brain, which are essentially intui-

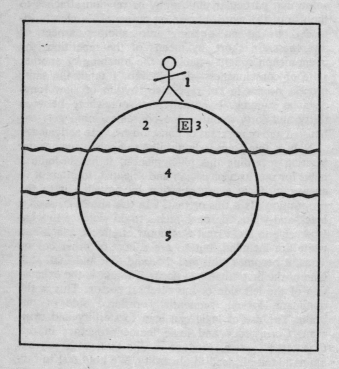

Figure 3

tive, aesthetic, creative, nonlogical and nonsequential and which seem to escape the temporal order of things.

I am hard pressed to say where consciousness then lies, because at the end of the run, as contrasted with many drug experiences, the memory of the encounter remains. This is also true of many meditative techniques. The right side of the brain seems to contain the neuronal machinery of our "soul." The left side is the bricks-and-mortar aspect of how we function.

Another "that" which seems to occur is related to a deeper function of man. And here I must once again borrow from the theories of Jung, Freud, mystics and saints to attempt to explain this aspect. In Figure 3 the entire circle represents all of me, or you, as an individual. The tiny figure at No. 1 represents your image to the world. In Jungian terms it is your persona, your uniform. We all have many personae. And we often change our behavior to fit our various masks. The word "persona" comes from the Latin for "mask," which was used by actors on the ancient stage and derived from the verb "to sound through." The actors wore masks to denote tragedy or comedy, and their voices sounded through them. Thus, the policeman may wake up a husband and father, put on his uniform and change his behavior accordingly. This is true of all of us. We change our roles to fit the occasion. Only, we hope, we do not fall into the error of thinking we *are* our roles.

At No. 2 we have our conscious awareness. That is, the things we seem to know vividly and clearly. At No. 3 we have our ego. And when we talk about "I" or "me," we refer to this small square box which is seated in consciousness. At No. 4 we have the realm of the personal unconscious. This is the area to which Freud paid particular attention. He felt that this was all there was to the personality and that this comprised forgotten or repressed elements from consciousness. It was a major discovery and a significant advance in our understanding of man. In the area of No. 5 we have the collective unconscious. Here is where Jung differed from Freud. He felt that there was a deeper layer to the unconscious that held a treasure trove of symbols he called archetypes. He felt that we were born with this unconscious equipment and that consciousness slowly evolved from the unconscious. It would be precisely from this area, the collective unconscious, that our three-million-year heritage as a running animal would be represented. The collective unconscious is the collective experience of the species. It is where, within each of us, the symbolic memories of all our ancestors are collected. So that within me is the internal representation of a free-running, myth-making, roving, hunter-killer ape. The recent period—i.e., last five thousand years—of civilization are laid upon this deep structure as a thin veneer.

The collective unconscious is that inner caldron of deep drives and forces that provide us with many of our most striking and meaningful personal experiences. It is also the source of our creative energy. The collective unconscious is, in one sense, filled with many such wonderful figures. We project our political hopes onto men like John F. Kennedy and our more symbolic meaning onto other external events. I used to see my grandfather stand tall and erect, and cry, when they played the Polish National Anthem in church after Mass. I am able to recognize a similar feeling in myself when I hear the "Marine Corps Hymn." Both are really just external events, but they have resonated and stirred our souls deeply within. To another person they might appear as sentimental nonsense, or even dangerous feelings. For these feelings are so powerful that we "know" of their danger. The Germans who followed Hitler into World War II lost their sense of perspective, just as we are worried about our children in their choice of whom they will love. I hope the slogan "Love is blind" makes a bit more sense after this little discourse.

Psychological Effects

I feel that slow long-distance running does something to the established structure of the personality. It seems to weaken, alter or temporarily loosen the double barriers to the collective unconscious. The conditions necessary to this loosening are doubtless different for each person, but in my experience the following criteria seem either to facilitate or to inhibit penetration into one's inner world. Perhaps an annotated list of examples will help, with each criterion marked as either negative or positive.

Negative	*Positive*
Competition	Inner-directed attention
New surroundings	Prayer, mantra or chant
Other people	Counting
Conversation	Familiar surroundings
Pain	Pain, after it has gone

Competition. If one competes, either in a race or against oneself, it seems to abolish this loosening. That's why I dislike the concept of "miles." Too many of us get into the mode, "Well, I ran two miles yesterday; I'll do two and a half today." This obsession with distance is destructive.

New Surroundings. Our attention is directed toward the unfamiliar environment. It's simply protective and necessary. We then don't have our attention within. This doesn't mean that running in new places isn't great fun.

Other People. Here a social aspect predominates. We may have some absolutely delightful interpersonal experiences while running. The conversations may be a little crazy, but that's okay, it's part of the letting go. But, once again, our attention is directed to the other person and to our interaction with that person.

Conversation. This is partly the same as "other people"; but having a conversation with oneself can also inhibit the loosening process. I once ran with a kid in a marathon who talked to himself the entire way. He talked so much he didn't finish the marathon. Many people carry on this active inner dialogue with their mouths shut, with the same negative results.

Inner-Directed Attention. Just put your attention on your physical self—your fat, your body, breathing, back, legs, sweat. Keep it idly wandering around inside. This will help.

Prayer. This works very nicely, especially if it is a prayer you've learned as a child. Most people have something like this, even if it's "Matthew, Mark, Luke and John, bless this bed I lie upon." If you have, say it over and over.

Counting. If you have never learned a prayer (or a mantra or chant), or have no preference for one, then try counting—count up to 100 or just count until you're silly with numbers.

Familiar Surroundings. Find a running route that is safe and familiar. Be careful of cars. You can get so dreamy in this state that you can become distracted and get hit. Try to run this safe route over and over— memorize it and eventually it will take you running. The other day coming up the hill to my home, I had the feeling that I was standing still and was just pushing the earth past me until I rolled up the road and my house came into view. It was like a giant treadmill.

Pain. Initially pain is something that severely distracts our attention. We are taught to "get away" from pain. If you are to do the loosening process with the best possible result, I'd advise focusing your attention on the pain. Think of it, focus on it, consider it, find the edges of your pain, label it—e.g., sharp, dull, throbbing, aching. Keep looking at it with your inner eye. You'll need some judicious handling of this so you won't hurt yourself. First be certain you are within your target rate. If you have a cardiovascular problem and the pain is anywhere in your chest or arms or neck, stop running and get checked out by your cardiologist. But if you are not a cardiac and are within your target rate, you know you are safe as far as your heart is concerned. Second, if you are dizzy, stop running. This is especially dangerous if it's hot out. It's one of the first signs of heat exhaustion and can lead to heat stroke. Third, if you feel a snapping or popping in your working muscles, stop. It could mean you've broken a small bone or torn a muscle or tendon. If none of these conditions prevails, you can probably "run through" the pain. Side pains are the most common. The other day I had a wonderful run with a headache. It was a nice, deep, throbbing headache located between my eyes, about a half inch within, and it wanted to spread out and get my eyes and the rest of my head. I kept looking at it for an hour's run and it finally gave up and left me, just as I got home and started to take a shower.

Now, all of these little gimmicks or tricks may or may not help. You'll probably discover something for yourself that works best for you. The whole vein of this is to attempt to loosen the barriers between your consciousness and the personal and collective unconscious. If all goes well, you will begin to resonate with your own self, and the experience will be delightful. You may even be touching aspects of your archetypes, in a relatively safe way. The archetypes are representations of many different symbols, and we sometimes experience them while awake as religious experiences, or in dreams as powerful and significant dreams, or in psychosis, where they overwhelm the ego. As I enter this realm of psychology, science and religion, I realize that these descriptions raise more questions than they answer and seem pretty far afield from jogging. So I will try—briefly and therefore inadequately—to explain the connection between these models of man and what happens at certain times during the process of slow long-distance running.

It is my contention that, just as prayer, meditation, dream analysis and some drug experiences open doors into these areas not usually accessible to us, under the appropriate circumstances slow long-distance running opens similar doors. The subjective experience of the runner appears the same, and he becomes revitalized or reenergized in a psychological or spiritual or creative sense. The key to the process is the length of the run and certain attitudes of the runner. Just as people seem to need to learn how to meditate or pray, they need to learn how to run in this manner—both externally and inside their own minds. And, just as in prayer or meditation, it doesn't always work, or it seems to work to varying degrees.

The stimulus may be external and therefore triggered by perceptual mechanisms such as vision, smell or sound, or it may be wholly internal and arise from the personal or collective unconscious. In addition, I have encountered certain running individuals who seem to have reached out of the circle postulated in Figure 3 into the realm that we usually call religious or mystical experience. Particular characteristics of the various types of experiences are as follows: if the experience is just perceptual, the runner may be willing to share it—but only with someone he trusts; we usually do not want those around us to think we are odd. If the experience penetrates the realm of the personal unconscious (No. 4 in the diagram), the experiencer usually keeps it to himself, unless he is deliberately guided to use it in therapy with an understanding therapist. If there is a penetration of the collective unconscious (No. 5), the individual never really forgets the experience. It is vivid and has the quality of an outstanding personal event in his life. He knows it is subjective and seldom risks sharing it with anyone. Finally, if the experience goes beyond the confines of the hypothetical circle, either he may mistrust what happened to him and try to forget it, or it is likely to change his life in a significant manner. This change will usually be one in life-style, and the individual will himself identify it as a moral or religious change. If the individual continues to run and experience this particular phenomenon, he may describe it as an external demand, which he "must" follow. And he can find personal comfort only when he accomplishes this change.

As you see, I make no clear distinctions between the body, mind and soul. In fact, I am not able to do so. I find I am comfortable with the idea that a steady state of cardiovascular functioning may somehow, in a way yet unknown to us, trigger the neurohumoral mechanisms that allow us to have experiences that are genuinely religious. I am equally comfortable with the idea that each individual needs to find his own soul and counteract the detrimental effects of urban life. In fact, it even seems sensible to attempt to resonate with our three-million-year heritage and to stimulate our bodies, whatever our age and condition, to function to their best. And it appears that this process of resonating with our biological heritage may open internal doors within ourselves that we had not known were there. The running itself does not supply any answers. It is like an alarm clock, a sign, a symbol, perhaps like a stoplight changing from red to green. It seems to allow the vehicle of the soul to go forward at least for a while.

The ideas and statements that come from this other area of our consciousness often appear strongly contradictory. I think it is dangerous, in listening to that inner voice, to believe and take action upon every message that penetrates. It is safer just to listen. And to note the contradictions and paradoxes. Eventually, these will be resolved. A course of action, the change in life-style will seem to unfold.

There is a great desire in many of us to force an issue, to try to change ourselves by an act of willpower. Divert that desire or drive into running; harness that particular energy to the basic running formula, and many times this will use up all your conscious desire to force things. Get up, run, do the pattern and let the rest flow. Let it be like a river, a fountain, a spring. Listen inwardly.

For example, in discussing the collective unconscious, we assume that we are not born an empty organism, or a tabula rasa to be written upon by our personal environment or to be manipulated by culture, circumstance or behavior modification. In this particular concept of ourselves, we can conceive of that deep realm of the unconscious like a hidden treasure room. In it are stored a vast array of symbols, perhaps like the tarot deck, which can have particular meanings for us individually. Apparently no two people have the same deck of cards; no one treasure room is really identical to another.

Somehow, just about everyone is aware of his or her own sense of inner discontent, a small voice that says, "I'm missing something." Many people then try to solve that by external acquisition and achieve only an odd sense of disappointment. Listen to the other side of your mind. As you read, let your mind wander. Let it filter through to the other side, that side that knows what to pick up, knows which bits and pieces are true and apply to you where you are now. This running therapy program is somewhere between logic and intuition. The whole scientific part of this program is based on logic—good, Western, scientific, pedantic, organized, statistical, cold, factual, vectored, purposive, goal-oriented and directed. But it is a dull world then. It has no surprises. No art. No fun. You will be a dropout.

The other side. The right side of the brain, where intuition breathes and lives and tells us that clock time isn't true, that flowers, colors, love, poetry, music and "something else" just beyond our knowing do exist—if not smothered and overwhelmed by logic, the Apollonian. So let the right brain in. Let intuition have her say in this business. Let her look within you and out at others and at what you read, see, hear and feel. It will embellish your running and open new gates. As you practice allowing that talent to develop, new dimensions will unfold. When to run fast. When slow. Pacing. Sleep. Easing. Making love. Being lazy. Being full. He, she, it provides the balance. In one way this technique, if I can call it that, is a way to achieve an internal acquisition. Certainly it is a way to a better heart, a healthier body and a hope of finding your own individual personal meaning and significance.

8

Running and Therapy

PSYCHOTHERAPY

AFTER I HAD BEEN RUNNING for about four months, the idea occurred to me one day while running that, if the positive effects I had noticed on myself and the cardiacs were so clear, I should involve a group of my patients in running. I was fairly adept in the use of group therapy. I had begun using it in 1959 and have used it in many forms ever since. I carried out some of the initial clinical research on married-couples group therapy in the early 1960's. I have had groups both large and small, specialized (like married couples or schizophrenics), mixed groups, confrontation groups, supportive groups. But my overall concept of group therapy was that it was an indoor, essentially sedentary activity. While in some group endeavors, certain trips might be taken, such as to plays, and in some other group processes the group might visit someone's home to see and feel the environment, and in still other groups, especially family-group therapies, the therapist might spend a weekend in the home of the family both as observer and therapist, I had never heard of a group

126

process that involved running. In spite of my considerable professional knowledge of group therapy, I was at a loss as to what to do. But I also felt comfortable in the role of a group therapist and I did not feel that I would be harming my patients, so I proceeded to assemble a group. This group consisted of seven of us, of mixed sexes and a wide variety of so-called problems including depression, addiction, schizophrenia, anxiety, and anorexia nervosa.

Usually there is a distinct difference between the patient and the therapist. This difference is reinforced in many ways. The patient comes to the therapist for help. The patient pays the therapist. The therapist has spent an astonishing number of years being trained: medical school, internship, residency, analysis, further training. This distancing sometimes helps, but very often I believe it seriously hinders the process of therapy, for I have learned that the significant changes in therapy occur in the unconscious of both the patient and the therapist. Freud, for example, evolved the technique of psychoanalysis, in which the patient lies on a couch and attempts to free-associate. The therapist is able to see the patient, but the patient cannot see the therapist. This was the way Freud attempted to free the patient from his inhibitions, and to reduce further the influence of the therapist by not having him visible. Freud found it didn't quite work that way, and discovered that the attitude of the therapist toward the patient did communicate itself through a process known as countertransference. Jung sat facing his patients, and according to reports from people he treated, he was much more open and responsive to his patients. It didn't appear to hinder the process of therapy in any significant way. In fact, it seemed to help it along.

Now there were friends and analysands of Freud who would take walks with him in the Vienna woods. They would have chats about the unconscious and it was considered analysis. But that seems to be the extent of the therapeutic physical activity on the part of

Freud. Jung practiced Yoga. He felt he had to do it to counterbalance the extreme preoccupation with the psychic side of life. In my own practice of psychotherapy, I had followed the usual model of the American psychiatrist. I tried to remain objective; I recognized the emergence of countertransference and treated this phenomenon in the usual way, which is first to attempt to work it out in myself, then to obtain consultative help from a colleague and thirdly (almost never) discuss it with the patient.

As you read all this, I hope you will see that there is a tedium of rules and structures that have insinuated themselves into the way a psychiatrist practices. In the so-called medical model of psychotherapy, the therapist is like a surgeon. You don't really care if the surgeon is an agnostic or a Republican, or if he had a hostile mother. You, as a patient, are only interested in his competence. He treats your ailment, be it a boil or an inflamed appendix, and his personal life is of secondary interest.

There are some psychiatrists who practice the same way. They "treat" their patients. The doctor *does* something *to* the patient. However, the word "therapy" has different connotations. It means "service" and implies doing something *with* the patient.

Of the two forms of psychotherapy, I have always tended toward the latter therapy model. To my own surprise and pleasure, the running therapy opened up a new therapeutic aspect. For as I ran along with my patients, my own unconscious was stimulated. And as we explored the meanings and stimuli for both the patient and therapist, it became quite evident that I could no longer adhere to any stereotyped rules as a therapist. I had to share my inner feelings, or my reticence was immediately perceived by the other group members and the entire process would bog down. My only reservations revolved around the concept of confidentiality. I did not feel that I could share material which was given to me in confidence. Thus, a new position became clear. My patients could ask me anything, and I would answer them as long as it did not violate the confidence of someone else. Naturally, I would do this only if they, too, were held by the same rule or bonds concerning me.

The rules were quite simple. We met three times per week, ran together for one hour at 75 percent of our maximum cardiac output, and then met immediately afterward as a group for a second hour. The group was closed, which meant no new members were added without the permission of everyone in the group. We did have guests, but we didn't operate with our usual therapeutic intensity when they were around. The confidentiality was absolute and still remains in force, so that I must refrain from the usual case-study approach in pleasant deference to that one of our few rules.

I hold this first group very dear to my soul. With one another we explored the new psychic territories that appeared in front of us. Together we noticed that we all changed our life habits at differing rates and paces. Smoking decreased, then stopped for one. Drinking followed the same pattern. My obesity fell away. Depressions lifted. Destructive relationships were ended by improvement or by separation. Excessively bizarre thought processes were eliminated without destroying the verve and spontaneity of that person. New friends appeared. In short, the group was successful, and the combination of running and therapy seemed to be the key. One member was not helped and dropped out of the group. That member had undergone electroshock treatment several years before, administered by a previous psychiatrist, which may have made the difference.

This first group is now formally disbanded. There has been a research-group design that ran for seven months at San Diego State University, and another therapeutic group is currently formed.

From these experiences and my own couple of thousand hours of therapeutic running, I have been led to the following concepts. These ideas may change as I continue to work with this new modality, but it is where I am at the present time.

It seems that man's soul has always been troubled. Perhaps it is because we are able to see the approach of our own deaths and we wish to be immortal. We do not accept death, at least in the Occident, with ease or grace. We strive to be remembered, and our religions often tell us we are able to live forever.

The shaman, witch doctor, priest—all combined the roles of doctor-psychotherapist and priest into one. In the rock wall-paintings of prehistoric man, we can project backward into time and assume that even then man's soul was troubled. He fought against the demons of disease and death, and against the mysterious powers of nature.

And then rational man emerged. His basic premise was disbelief. His tool was hard skepticism. His vision was austerity itself. And from this posture we have achieved antibiotics and television and automobiles and machines and space flight.

Prominent scientists of all ages have spurred us on in our revulsion against excesses of blind belief. Copernicus told us that the earth revolved around the sun; men then felt that this meant we were not the center of the universe. Darwin clarified the principles of evolution, and men then interpreted this to mean that we were not the special creatures of God. Freud demonstrated the strength and presence of the unconscious, and men then got the idea that this abolished individual freedom. We then turned the sharp blade of rational dissection upon the human soul.

Reason, logic and science teamed up to probe inner space. And they were met with an unusual resistance. The inner regions of man were mysterious and could not be fully apprehended by the available tools provided by reason, logic and science. The major problem remained. We were studying ourselves and were unable to be fully objective.

At the age of forty-two, I had found myself a member of that cult which attempted to fill the shoes of the shaman, priest and physician. I found that this was an acceptable role for me. I was to be reflective, thoughtful, intelligent, well versed in the various aspects of my prefession, slightly mysterious and allowed to have minor idiosyncrasies; and I was to be . . . sedentary. My patients were to come to me in my office and sit and talk for 50 minutes. The total amount of my activity was getting up and down out of my chair every 50 minutes. And I was expected to retain my professional posture for at least eight to twelve hours a day for five to six days a week.

A Martian would notice something rather strange about my existence. The tensions in the air of the operating theater of the therapist's office were often highly charged. The emotional voltage was in the kilowatt range. But the physical outlet of energy was in the microerg category. At least shamans danced, priests moved about at their ceremonies, but the psychotherapist was sedentary (psychiatrists have the highest suicide rate of any professional group in the United States).

In this new therapeutic role, I was doing something markedly different. I was directly participating in the action with the patient—we were both running. And we experienced similar phenomena—pain, the high, the altered states after 40 minutes. If I compare this technique of therapy with dream analysis, it's like dreaming the same dream as the patient at the same time. The therapy was immediate. The nuances were immediately available and my own unconscious was more visible to me and to my patients. At times, it seemed as if the archetypes within us rose up to consciousness and lived and talked as we ran along. If someone looked at us, he would see only a small group of people running slowly, together, or in twos, threes or alone. If that especially sensitive Martian could look in now, he would see a resonance between the physical energy and the flowering of new colors in the soul.

This type of running therapy also highlighted a special feature of what we define as "normal" or "abnormal." These terms are culturally and historically relative. The society sets the norm. Thus, believing in witches and burning them alive is considered abnormal by today's society. A few hundred years ago it was normal. Following this same logic, we are able to understand cross-cultural deviances. Thus, in one culture everyone "sees" the Virgin in the corner of the church on a particular day. An outside visitor does not see her. If he is wise, he will pretend to see her. If he lives there long enough, he will see her too, without pretending. It's horrifying to imagine what "normal" would mean today if the Nazis had won World War II.

Thus, sanity and insanity and politics and culture are all of the same tree.

In this form of therapy, the role of the individual seemed more elevated. But not with the passion that demanded that the culture be changed or altered. At times the culture was defined like a freeway or tollway—potentially lethal if you abused its rules, but not a personal agent directed against your own freedom or comfort.

When we dealt with the world "out there," with its rules, institutions, idiocies and contradictions, it was with a kind of wonder. As a group we would often conspire to help a particular member cope with the machinery of things like school, money, divorce, children, illness, sex, automobiles and taxes. We saw these outside agents as neither hostile nor friendly. They could be lethal or helpful—just as water can drown or revive a man dying of thirst.

The focus lay in the inner core of that person. It dwelt, in a gentle way, around that center, knowing that it was in that special center that ease and meaning and fun and purpose could be found. Strangely we, outside, could never know the exact dimensions of that center. It was too mobile and too sacred for it to be subject to the intense focus of interest, even though that interest was one of love.

I began to believe, in a shy way at first, that somehow we had discovered a new form of therapy. It was biologically based. It focused on the cardiovascular system. The changes occurred physiologically from the inside out. It also seemed based on the genetic heritage of man—man the slow long-distance runner. And finally, it appeared to focus on man as an individual and especially on man as an individual in spite of the accident of his culture and the time of his birth. It fostered analysis. It helped the individual discover new depths within himself. The term "paleoanalytic psychology" seemed to fit best of all, or "paleoanalysis." If this concept is correct, then it should resonate with the spontaneously discovered attempts of man to help himself. I have talked to many runners—runners who run long, medium and short distances—and I have come to the conclusion that running, done in a particular way, is a form of natural psychotherapy. It stimulates the unconscious and is a powerful catalyst to the individual psyche. The catalyst aspect I have covered in the preceding chapter, "Theory."

One of the biggest problems in therapy is the analyst himself. Too often, he may be unaware of the complexities of the patient-therapist dyad and may impede the development of the unconscious of the patient. The therapist himself should be a catalyst. His role should be similar to that of the alchemist's assistant. The colorful and often wonderful developments that occur in the alchemical laboratory of his patient's soul are not directly the result of the therapist's efforts. He merely facilitates the process of growth and change brought about by a natural series of events.

The therapist should also have some familiarity with the various journeys experienced by himself and others, so that he may be able to give a hint or two as to what may be happening in the inner world of his patient. An example of the therapist as catalyst may help to clarify. A forty-year-old professor of education had the following dream. He was in a large airplane, like a 747, and it had landed in his hometown. All the passengers left, but the stewardesses remained. One of them looked very attractive and, to his surprise, came up to him and asked if they could make love. She complained that, although she wanted to make love, there were no appropriate places to do so. The man then said, "Well, why not do it right here in the aisle?" All the other stewardesses gathered around and encouraged the girl and teased the man—that he would be incapable of doing it in public. The man responded with good humor and proceeded to make love to the girl.

Now it would be impossible to interpret this dream without a full and thorough knowledge of this man's past and of his present circumstances. His therapist knew that he had always been an intelligent and active man, but his creativity seemed thwarted. The patient was ashamed of his dream. He feared it meant he was unfaithful to his wife or was sexually deviant. The analyst's interpretation was that the girl was his anima. The other girls were ladies-in-waiting, like a queen's. Landing meant that he had come down from the clouds and was on solid earth, at home. The sexual act was one of creativity, a true loving and creative act. The fact that it was done in public meant that finally some portion of the external world was going to see the products of this union. The dream was saying that he was not going to hide his light under a bushel any longer. He was going to "go public," and his thwarted creativity would emerge and be recognized. Within two months of this dream and its interpretation, he started writing a book, which was later accepted for publication.

The timing of the interpretation and its integration with the actual situation of the patient is critical. And the value of the interpretation may be judged only by its effect upon the patient with the passage of time.

The significant questions to ask are these: Did it help develop the inner qualities of the patient? Did it free him further? Did it lead him to explore new dimensions of himself? If this does not happen, then the analyst must be ready to abandon his notions and see if there was something he missed. So the final judge of therapy is the patient.

There are some natural protections against certain potentially detrimental effects of therapy. One of these is the patient's fear of losing his own individuality. In actual fact this is an impossibility. The patient may respect, emulate and/or love the therapist. However, as the particular characteristics of the therapist are passed along to the patient, they are in themselves changed by the patient in subtle ways. Those characteristics then become the patient's, and indeed he has only increased the general range of his own resources. It is impossible to become someone else. No matter how hard we try to do so, we remain ourselves permanently.

Another aspect of therapy, and perhaps of life itself, is the way we deal with that strange delusion of the ego that it has the power to change things. The ego, the center of our consciousness, keeps thinking that it is in charge of the whole personality and is somehow able, usually by efforts called willpower or some other such force, to change other people around itself and some of the physical events in the world about us. This notion is supported by advertising agencies, politics, Newtonian mechanics, banks, schools and governments. However, even a brief look at the nature of things, such as the tides, the growth of a tree, the rotation of planets, how tall we are, all indicate that the nature of what goes on is perhaps closer to the concept of a river. We are all being carried along by the current. And the scenery changes. Some people imagine that they are actually doing the movement themselves. "Serendipity" perhaps means looking around and seeing what was there all the time. For example, penicillin was around for all of man's existence. It took the accidental observation of Alexander Fleming to bring it to our attention and use. It seems that major discoveries are made by looking idly about, perhaps out of the corners of the eye, not by staring straight ahead.

The focused staring, the use of blueprints, the attention to linear detail are also major tools of man. The slow development of minor refinements in technique preoccupy the majority of his time. This same process is also helpful in psychotherapy as the patient and analyst together begin to delineate the topography of that patient's unconscious. For example, in one patient, whenever he dreamed that he was going south on a trip, it usually meant that the content of the dream was more symbolic and more related to the collective unconscious than to his personal unconscious.

Therefore, a basic principle of this form of therapy is to look for the small clues and hints that show up in individual conscious behavior that lead us into the more significant and richer realm of the unconscious. The running aspect of therapy appears to stimulate these openings into the unconscious and is a valuable tool in the therapeutic process.

THE RUNNING THERAPIST

The therapist who uses this modality should be specifically trained in the unique aspects of change that occur in people in this process. He has to be a runner himself and has to be a good therapist, able to integrate these two aspects right on the field. He should have a firm grasp of the principles of cardiovascular functioning, diet and all the things that are covered in this book. He must run with his groups, freely willing to be a collateral member of the group. His leadership should evolve from demonstrated and accepted knowledge and love, not from authority, status or position. I am currently training a small group of professional people in this new modality. The problem to date has been the split in academic circles between those who are trained in organic or physiological modalities and those who are trained only in a psychological manner. Someone trained solely in the physiological aspect may not be able to appreciate the emergence of certain clues that are emotional. For example, one man whom I know quite well undergoes a shift in his basic personality orientation when he gets into a long-distance run. When he isn't running, he is a taciturn, cryptic, nonverbal, dour introvert. After he passes 10 miles, he becomes a talkative, verbal, extroverted, playful man. When his personality shifts in this way, he will often discuss both his problems and his hidden aspirations. In his normal, nonrunning personality he would never even begin to approach these subjects. These openings are therapeutic opportunities and can be best employed or discussed while running with the patient.

If the focus of the therapist is primarily psychological, he will not be able to give appropriate advice concerning diet, stretching exercises, cardiovascular factors, running style, shoes, and so on.

Thus, in this training I have required the people involved to be familiar with both areas. The best way for them to learn the physiological aspect is for them to train for a marathon. While they train themselves, they learn a great deal about themselves and physiology. The psychological aspects are covered by regular seminars, with a focus on Jungian psychology, and work with patients who are in the running-therapy program.

DEPRESSION

Depression is perhaps the most common disease of our age. If we examine some of our American cultural patterns, we are able to see that popular music, especially country and western, has as its major theme one of loss, sorrow, and naturally depression—for example, "On Top of Old Smokey," where the singer has lost his true love. The melodies of many of our popular songs are thinly disguised wailings, sobs and other expressions of sorrow. We have very few "war songs" (contrast American Indian songs), songs of ritual passage such as puberty, marriage, birth and adulthood, although the penetrating depressive theme can latch onto virtually any of these topics.

Thus, when discussing depression, we must first examine the cultural matrix within which the symptoms occur. In certain contexts, especially those of loss, depression is tacitly accepted. Generally speaking, at the present time depression is more "allowed" or "accepted" in women than in men. The stereotyped roles of male and female do not allow a man to cry openly or to be depressed without cause. In a patronizing way women are even expected to be depressed; it is usually attributed to their biology, and they are excused and humored for their weakness. For males this experience is not accepted and may have a connection with the high suicide rate among men.

Freud differentiated between depression and mourning, and also identified the similarities in his work *Mourning and Melancholia*. Since that was published, there has been a monumental amount of work done on depression.

Depression itself is characterized by both physical and emotional symptoms. The physical ones are called signs, for one can see them happen in the other person. The emotional ones are called symptoms, for they are reported by the person himself.

Under the category of signs are psychomotor retardation, insomnia (especially early-morning awakening insomnia), weight loss or weight gain, constipation, a sad-appearing face, halitosis (due to decreased salivation), reddened eyelids and crying. The symptoms include hopelessness, loneliness, a sense of internal agitation, obsessive worrying about a particular subject, sadness, fear and dejection. Thus, there are physical as well as emotional aspects of depression. Recent work in the area of psychobiology has produced some new information about depression. For example, some depressive patterns appear to be hereditary. In addition, we now have available to us some medications such as the antidepressants (tricyclic compounds, monoamine oxidase inhibitors and lithium salts) which are occasionally helpful in the clinical treatment and management of depression. However, no symptom as ubiquitous as depression can have its existence noted in man without our asking whether depression has a functional purpose.

There are many clues that there is a functional, or purposeful, aspect to depression. We find depressions often appearing as the first symptoms of a serious physical illness. We also see depressions following certain crises, such as an illness or surgery, childbirth, a promotion, graduation, and so on. It seems as if the soul of man has to give itself time to reorganize and reestablish its forces, and the depression that occurs in these latter circumstances seems to point in that direction. I personally do not feel that all depressions are bad and have to be removed by whatever form of therapy available. The soul, or psyche, of that individual may be undergoing a necessary time of readjustment or restructuring and the internal work is reflected by the symptom we call depression.

However, there is a tendency for some depressions to become habitual, and they can disable. A person constantly in the grip of those wretched feelings has a poor chance of utilizing the resources of the other parts of his personality, or the resources of the therapist. It is at this point that I began to use antidepressant medication. However, the problems with medication are these: (1) it fosters dependency upon the therapist and the medication; and (2) it is an unnatural, foreign intrusion upon the biochemistry of that individual. It would be much better if the therapist had a means of temporarily alleviating depression without the introduction of medication. Here is where I have been able to use running as an extremely useful therapeutic tool in the treatment of depression.

Ms. W., a thirty-four-year-old woman, entered therapy with the chief complaint of depression. It was necessary in the very early stages of analysis to use the tricyclic antidepressants to help her through the near-paralyzing effects of her depression. As the analysis progressed, the activities of her current and past life and the topography of her unconscious revealed that she had a wonderfully rich unconscious and a decided artistic talent. However, her creativity and her tendency to be depressed had common roots. Thus, to obliterate her depression fully might also have endangered her capacity to be creative. The medication proved to foster dependency, which would also be an unfavorable result of her analysis. In her case, the running aspect of therapy provided the answer. Soon after starting to run, she no longer needed the antidepressants. As time progressed, she found that she herself could run and alleviate her depression as she chose to. She no longer sees me in analysis and her life is, for her, more gratifying and successful than before. She is not free of being depressed at times, but when this symptom becomes troublesome for her, she alleviates it by an hour's run.

It is extremely gratifying to a therapist to see such a result. Perhaps more important was to see how the running aspect acted as a catalyst both for her and for other patients. A typical experience would be that the patient would come to the running session in a clearly dejected, nonverbal, depressed mood. As the run progressed, he would become more verbal, more open. At the end of the hour very active therapy can take place. An important part of the therapeutic technique is the immediacy of the sit-and-talk part of the therapy after the run. Therapist and patient should stay together. A break to change clothing or shower will disrupt the flow of openness and separate the two aspects of the therapy, to everyone's loss.

One of the important symptoms of depression to watch in this form of therapy is the insomnia. As I mentioned above, early-morning awakening is a sign of depression. It is also especially dangerous, as it is often correlated with suicidal behavior.

Slow, long-distance running itself, in normal people, produces an insomnia. It is not constant and, unlike the insomnia of depression, does not bother the individual. One of the interesting effects of the running aspect of this form of therapy on the depressed individual is that the insomnia typical of that patient's depression will gradually disappear. Also, his sleep pattern will change. He will sleep more lightly, dream more, and awaken more refreshed in the morning. The typical depressed individual wakes up too early, tosses and turns, feels fretful and exhausted in the morning. It is important for the therapist to recognize these shifts and help explain them to the patient.

One probable reason for this particular shift in sleep pattern has to do with the function of dreams. Each night the soul attempts to repair itself in sleep. If, however, the person is deeply troubled, either within himself or due to external circumstances, his dreams can be repressed. The ego sees the dream as another meddlesome intrusion upon an already rocking boat. Thus, the first step most people take is to try to override the dream aspect. They will complain bitterly of the insomnia and may use sleeping medication, or drugs such as alcohol to help them through the night. They blame their fatigue on their insomnia. In fact, all they are doing is getting more out of touch with themselves.

The running reverses this process. The dreams do surface and can be brought into therapy. It's really fun to hear a patient who used to complain bitterly of insomnia report one day, "I didn't sleep last night, but it didn't bother me at all, and I feel just fine. In fact, I'm full of energy." This phenomenon is directly related to the running.

The theory to help account for this change is that the running, in ways not yet known, is related to sleep and the unconscious. I am of the opinion that the runner's insomnia is similar to the brain saying, "I've had my sleep today. I don't need any more." For many of the subjective feelings of long-distance runners are similar to those of sleep, as mentioned in the chapters "Psychological Effects" and "Theory."

An interesting effect of long-distance running is related to competition. Often following a marathon, one experiences a couple of days of mild depression. This is partly just the letdown and physiological depletion that occur when one has run 26 miles 385 yards. However, I have talked to runners who have experienced severe postmarathon depressions lasting several weeks. And in every instance the runner had completed a marathon in his personal best time (his personal record, or PR). During these discussions I find the following pattern: The runner wants to "break" a particular time—say 3½ hours, or 3 hours, or 2½ hours; it all depends on his previous ability and performance. Next he trains especially hard for that particular race. He points toward that race. He may begin training a year ahead of time, but usually he starts the really hard training three months before the race. Finally, during the race he is highly tense and keyed up. (Just before, he is apt to be irritable and straining to go; and then during the race itself he drives himself without stint.) When he finishes, you can usually see the agony in his face. The entire race is an internal measuring of saving and expending energy and of rigorous adherence to a time schedule. It is just this person who is vulnerable to the postmarathon depression. Perhaps it is in a small way similar to the famous depression felt by Alexander the Great when, as legend has it, he mourned that there were no new worlds to conquer.

At any rate, the depression is real and can have some after-effects. A thirty-year-old runner who had run a marathon in about 2½ hours told me he would never run one again, "because I know I couldn't ever do better than that, and if I didn't do it, I'd feel terrible." And a forty-seven-year-old marathoner told me after the Santa Monica Marathon, "Well, I'm not going down. I'm still in the same bracket. Best time I ever did." And a woman runner told me, "If I don't do as well as I did before, everyone will know and I'll be embarrassed." They are all trapped in the competition business, and depression appears linked to that attitude. It's simple enough to remedy this if you do run marathons. Deliberately plan to run a few marathons very slowly. Enjoy them, make them fun runs. And if once into a run you feel faster, then let your feelings be your guide.

There is another therapeutic technique for those who are trapped by circumstance into being highly visible and are encouraged to compete by the hero-hungry public. And that is to plan for the postmarathon depression, after pointing for the one good race in a year: Deliberately cultivate the symptoms. Take several days off. Don't run or be active. Lie about. Eat whatever you want and as much as you want. In other words, ride with this particular wave.

It's hard to give general advice at this point because of the differences between people. With some, it's necessary to employ active forms of analytic therapy and sometimes medication to keep the depression from settling in for a long siege.

SCHIZOPHRENIA

Schizophrenia is one of the most complicated and difficult diseases to treat in medicine. There is a worldwide, cross-cultural incidence of this disease, which affects 1 percent of the earth's population. It's probably not a single disease, either, and it has many different forms, such as paranoid schizophrenia, simple schizophrenia and hebephrenic schizophrenia. It is marked by difficulty in interpersonal relationships, withdrawal or paranoia and disorganization of behavior. When the patient becomes disorganized, hospitalization may be necessary. His emotional state often appears bizarre, as he may be responding to an internal world which produces hallucinations. His thinking may be seriously disturbed. In many ways, the patient seems overwhelmed by the contents of the unconscious, and his ability to manage external reality and his own inner world has broken down.

I have been working with patients with this terrible disease now for twenty years. My first patient, as a medical student on the psychiatric service in 1955, was a schizophrenic. Since then I have seen many schizophrenics. I have used all of the treatment modalities available to me, and I have gained an increased respect for the tenacity of this disease, its multiple symptoms, the pain it causes the patient and his family.

In the past twenty years the use of antipsychotic medications has helped a great deal in the management and treatment of schizophrenia. Also, carefully applied psychotherapy works well in conjunction with medication.

I have now had experience using the running model in conjunction with patients who have schizophrenia. Frankly, I have been amazed at the result. The trouble is that my sample is too small to be of statistical significance. And I am unable to separate out the factor of my own enthusiasm, which often affects the outcome of a treatment modality. At any rate, with all these caveats, I have now had the delightful experience of working with schizophrenic patients, using this form of running therapy, and have seen them change dramatically. They begin to lose their symptoms; medication can be reduced and often discontinued; and they have picked up the course of their lives until several are no longer recognizable as schizophrenics at all—even by professional observers.

I want to emphasize that this result may be due to other factors, even the extra attention paid to the patients. I do not feel that slow long-distance running is a cure for schizophrenia. I'm only reporting an interesting result and one that continues to occupy my attention.

ANOREXIA NERVOSA

Anorexia nervosa is a disease, usually of young women (though an occasional young man does have it), that is characterized by a preoccupation with food but a marked reduction in food intake to the point of starvation and even death. The patient becomes thinner and finally emaciated. Hospitalization with tube feeding is then necessary to prevent death. Patients show few other symptoms that are distinctly emotional. Often they love to exercise and will exercise at every opportunity.

One such young person became a patient of mine. His/her weight had dropped so low that hospitalization and tube feeding were required twice as lifesaving procedures. This person was finally placed in my running-therapy program. Initially he/she showed great enthusiasm and was an avid runner. After a few months the enthusiasm dropped off as weight gain occurred. Secondary symptoms, such as the preoccupation with food, stopped; weight went from 90 to 120 pounds; and he/she stopped running, because he/she felt weight gain was correlated with the running. Other factors in this patient's personality associated with this disease also changed, and the therapeutic result was quite satisfactory for the patient and for me.

Again, the same concepts and questions arise as with schizophrenia, except that here I employed a symptom favored by the person. It sounds strange, doesn't it—running as a therapeutic help in the treatment of anorexia nervosa? Again, it was employed with individual and group psychotherapy.

LIFE-STYLE CHANGES

One interesting comment on the process of psychotherapy is that any really competent psychotherapist stops seeing his patients as "sick" very shortly after beginning his therapy. He is often able to see certain aspects of the person's life-style that act as focal points for his difficulty. The resultant symptoms seem to spring from these focal areas, and these repetitive patterns often appear so habitual that they embody a life-style.

A case history may help here. This is the story of a man fifty years of age who came in with the complaint of depression. He was a highly successful and respected professional man in his community. His symptoms of depression were related to excessive drinking. About once a fortnight he would get seriously drunk and become belligerent and ill.

Now to trace certain aspects of his life to his personal past. As a child and adult, he was very anxious to please, in fact, overly so. His father had been harsh and cold. He desired warmth and approval from anyone. Thus, at school he was an excellent student and advanced rapidly. As an adult he was regarded as the stabilizing force on many committees and boards—a kind and generous man.

His father drank heavily. And he, too, began drinking in his late teens. As age increased, he slowly increased his drinking. When he was forty-two, his wife had an affair, which she confessed to him. She was not an affectionate woman and they had some marital counseling at that point, which seemed to patch up the marriage. However, the sequelae were overwhelming guilt on her part, which she handled by repressing all her sexual responses, including those toward her husband. The effect on him was confirmation of his deepest inner fears and insecurity, and he developed impotence and a fear that he might be homosexual. He responded by taking on more professional and community tasks, and the episodic drinking helped medicate and partially release the inner turmoil and conflict.

This story has the ring of many cases presented in analytic conferences and the usual factors—transference, countertransference, medication—were all present. However, there were several other factors that I could not answer by treating this man solely in the confines of my office. First, he was a prime candidate for a coronary. From his own viewpoint he had little to live for. And his internist confirmed my fears, for his blood pressure was rising to dangerous levels. The second reality was that in spite of marked professional success, he did not feel a personal sense of achievement. The reason for this was that his professional success had been in response to the desire to please someone else. Therefore, to encourage him to greater professional efforts would only defeat what we were trying to do.

He entered analysis, but in addition he began running at 75 percent of his maximum cardiac output three times a week—individually rather than in a group. As time progressed, the behavior patterns began to change. His drinking lessened. His impotence was not absolute, and finally, he became addicted to running. The final changes occurred when he successfully completed a marathon. Here was an area where he had done it himself, and clearly so. For, although it became clear in the analysis that he began running just to please me, he soon found that that motivation wasn't enough to carry him through. It was when he was alone, with himself finishing his first marathon at fifty-one, that he got that special feeling of doing it for himself. Because it was quite evident that he did it alone. Now the life-style changes that took place were gradual and revolved around things like cutting his work schedule to allow himself more time for running, decreasing his drinking so he could run, altering his diet so he could adjust his body to the demands made upon it by the marathon training. These may seem simple, but in fact I feel they are the most important aspects of therapy. For insight without action only seems to reinforce the detrimental patterns of behavior.

Another example is that of a pleasant thirty-three-year-old woman who came into therapy complaining about her marriage. She was separated but wanted a reconciliation. She was honest and bright but was married to a man who was infantile in his relationships with her. He had temper tantrums, would verbally abuse her and treat her like a child; for example, giving her $20 a week to run the entire household when it was impossible to do so with the guests he brought home.

Again, in analysis, her dependency factors came into focus. She had been raised with the concept that the wife's role was to be passive. She had had one brief broken marriage and was fearful of losing this second husband. Soon enough she understood many of these factors. But, once again, there was something missing. Her parents were affluent and she had never, up to this age, had to face a problem that required a change in her own behavior; it was easier to change the surrounding world. In order to alter the marriage she had to show a greater internal strength, a kind of discipline. This was totally foreign to her.

Out on the running field she would often act like a small child. The most minor discomfort, the tiniest ache or pain, was magnified out of all proportion. With support and with some pushing, she soon realized that she could handle herself out there on the track. She developed what is usually called increased self-confidence. But to her, it was an inner knowledge that she could do things that were—or seemed to be—hard or foreign to her nature, or both. And she transferred that feeling to her marriage. Slowly her husband discovered that her passivity was gradually disappearing and she was occasionally opposing him. He threw a few tantrums and she emerged as the more sensible of the two.

The imbalance of her marriage was corrected and her personal marital goal was approached.

Again, it was in the running that she found her personal resources strengthened. Without it I doubt if she would have shown any progress.

Another case is that of Mr. J. W., a fifty-five-year-old man who lived in a rural Arkansas town. When he was fifteen, his father had died, and he had quit school to assume the responsibility of running his father's electrical-contracting business. He married his girlfriend at age sixteen and by age seventeen he had his first son. By the time he was twenty he was successfully running his family business and had a son and a daughter.

He moved to southern California in the 1950's and developed another electrical-contracting business, and over the years he became a successful builder and developer. He was quiet, honest, reliable, determined and dedicated to securing the financial position of his family.

After twenty years of marriage his wife became excessively religious. J. W. did not quarrel with her—he never learned to quarrel with a family member—but eventually their estrangement grew and he left home. He continued to visit her and his children.

He did not find another woman to comfort him; instead, he stepped up his business activities. His success grew, and two years before he walked into my office, he opened the biggest development project he had ever attempted. This was to be his final success, after which he felt he could devote some time to himself. Both children had finished college, had successful careers and were married.

His "final" business deal began to go awry a year before he saw me—ostensibly because of outside circumstances such as changes in building codes, environmentalist-group pressures, a partner who became ill. The problems seemed insoluble. He developed insomnia and became incapable of making any clear decisions. He had clear symptoms of a reactive depression.

It was apparent in the first two consultative sessions

that part of his difficulty was a life that had been lived almost totally for others. He had no hobbies, interests other than work or even any major sins. He had a rigid superego that was driving him onward. And he also had an unconscious that was rebelling against a lifetime of dreary work and "success." Finally, it was certain that, if he failed to rescue this project from defeat, he would lose all the financial gains he had made over the past thirty years or so.

Insight therapy was rather easy with him, but traditional psychotherapy, or analysis, wasn't enough. It was clear that he was a prime candidate for a coronary. He was tense, driven, depressed, caught in what appeared to be an insoluble dilemma. His blood lipids were elevated, as was his blood pressure. Therapy might help but in the meantime he might die of a coronary. In fact, it was clear to him and to me that if he did have a coronary he would be absolved from solving his problems, and at times he felt he preferred death to continuing. In addition, he was a very private and shy man—he could not accept the idea of working in a group. Thus, in one way, as a therapist, I was facing a crisis with this man. To ignore the physical factors, which were evident to me, would be derelict on my part.

Therefore, we agreed on a program that involved his meeting with me on a biweekly basis for traditional analytic work. In addition, after being appropriately stress-tested, he met with a running therapist (K-therapist) on an individual basis three times a week and was guided into the process of walking-running at his target rate. I met with the running therapist on a regular basis to discuss the progress of his therapy and, occasionally, all three of us would run together.

The result of this therapeutic approach was that he did not have a coronary and his blood pressure and blood lipids returned to normal. He has become much more familiar with his inner needs and is experiencing a bit of the childhood he missed. At age fifty-five he is learning to play. His running is a kind of play appropriately sanctioned by a physician. He has resolved his business problems and is currently reappraising his entire life-style. Without the addition of the running aspect of therapy, I doubt if this would have been the outcome.

MEDICATIONS

Mental-health programs, which use this form of running as a large group activity, usually have a significant number of patients who are on psychotropic medications. It is extremely important for the therapist to recognize that, if the running therapy is conducted properly, the need for medications decreases. Usually the first symptoms are the appearance of the toxic side effects of the various drugs. For, as the need decreases, the patient's present dosage is too much. Several of my patients were on considerable amounts of various psychotropic medications. Often the need for the medications continued to decrease until they were no longer necessary.

TIME EFFECTS

Eileen Waters and I were talking about how time changes for us while preparing for a marathon. We were to run a marathon a month from when we were chatting, and it seemed to us as if it were to occur in the next thirty seconds. The future was telescoped right into the next moment. Then we realized that a particularly strenuous run we had done together with Ozzie and Kip two days earlier seemed like two years before. So the past was stretched out oddly and as a result our subjective life-space sense was lengthened.

This conversation led me into some further observations of changes in subjective time sense that appear to be fairly common among long-distance runners. For example, one day a small group of us took a 3-hour run. We went out for 1½ hours and then turned back along the same track. As we returned, after we had run about 2 hours, we passed an area that helped us to recall our conversation on the way out. It seemed as if years had passed since that conversation. It was so long before as to feel old, and yet in clock time it happened within the past 2 hours.

Perhaps the most difficult aspect of the passage of subjective time is the first 20 to 30 minutes. It is in that period of time that we seem really locked into the metronome of clock time. It is slow, at times deadly slow. After 30 minutes, the slow crawl of time passes away and a new phase begins. This altered perception of time, at least of mechanical time, appears both faster and slower. Long involved thoughts can occur in minutes, and at other times whole chunks of clock time disappear. I recalled losing a half hour during one marathon. My memory bank was empty for that period. I discovered the loss when I checked my watch and thought it was wrong. It seemed to have leaped thirty minutes ahead. I forgot about it until I reached the finish line and saw ahead of me a kid of about fourteen whom I distinctly remembered seeing behind me. I never saw him go past, and yet there he was. I gather he passed me in that "blank" 30 minutes.

This alteration of the sensation of time can be used as a catalyst to examine our own rhythms of work, sleep, play, and so forth. Too often we become the programmed slaves to the passage of time, and our lives seem to disappear into a dwindling infinity, like the two railroad tracks that meet way ahead. As we get older, we begin to see people complain, in an amazed way, that time passes so quickly. Before they know it, their children are grown. They are gray and their friends are old. They are able to recall with nostalgia the utterly languid feeling of the endless time of childhood, either as a misery to live through a dull day at school, or with joy in anticipation of the time of summer vacation from June to Labor Day.

One of the subtle attractions of long-distance running is the change of this dwindling of subjective time. Our subjective time system is altered and we can be freed from that trap. Often the longest moment of a whole day occurs during some fragment of a morning run. It can remain there all day, towering above all the rest of that day's time. It is like a small, very precious jewel tucked away in my pocket.

PHYSICAL THERAPIES

Up to now in this chapter I have kept within my professional territory—my expertise as a psychotherapist. However, I feel it is necessary to refer to the interesting effect that running and diet have on certain specific diseases. It is also quite curious that a combination of exercise and a specific diet are helpful in all of these diseases. They are obesity, atherosclerosis, diabetes and hypertension.

If anyone has any of these disease entities, the program I am outlining below must be carried out under a physician's direction. It is necessary for the physician to adjust certain aspects of the program to the condition of the patient. For example, if a patient weighs 300 pounds or more, his legs and feet may not sustain his running for an hour at his target rate. He will have to walk for that hour until his weight is reduced and his leg muscles are strengthened. Another example in which the direct help of the physician is required to adjust the program relates to medication. If a patient has hypertension and is on medication to lower his blood pressure, his physician must work with the patient to adjust the dosage as the need for the medication is reduced. The same is true of diabetes.

There are two aspects to this method of helping in the natural treatment of these diseases—the exercise part and the diet part. The exercise aspect is close to what is advocated throughout the rest of this book, that is, running at your cardiovascular target rate for one hour three times a week. However, if you want to get results a bit faster, the way to do it is to add one hour of brisk walking on the days when you're not running. This means one hour a day, every day, with three days' running. It's also feasible to use another form of steady exercise on the nonrunning days, such as bicycling or swimming. Once again, the exercise pattern must be correlated to the individual, and it is mandatory that anyone with obesity, atherosclerosis, diabetes or hypertension, regardless of age, should not proceed with such a program until he has had a thorough stress test. For these conditions are all associated with an increased incidence of coronary heart disease.

The diet aspect should also be discussed with one's physician. There are two factors in the diet: the number of calories and the content of the diet. The caloric amount should be adjusted either to losing weight or to maintaining weight. To lose weight, a caloric amount of 1,500 calories per day should accomplish the purpose for most people. The content of the diet is where most people will have difficulty. However, it is possible to use this diet and be quite successful. There are certain specific foods and substances to avoid and other foods to use. The absolute avoidance list is as follows: tobacco in all forms, alcohol in all forms, coffee or tea, all sugars including honey, all fats, especially animal fats, all foods that contain cholesterol and all salt, whether added to food you cook or sprinkled on your food at the table. The foods that are helpful are fresh fruits, fresh vegetables and lean poultry.

Now I'd like to stop right here with this part of the program because you're probably telling yourself, "I can't eat anything!"—and you will be defeated before you begin. I can only tell you that this type of diet is not impossible but can actually be accomplished and give you good appetizing meals. But because of the wide range of individual tastes, and because it is so important to be successful, I would refer you to your physician, and he will either go over the diet program with you or refer you to a dietitian who will be able to adjust the meals to fit your particular taste patterns. There are several excellent references you can read, such as *Live Longer Now* by Leonard, Hofer and Pritikin (Grosset & Dunlap, 1974); *Modern Nutrition in Health and Disease*, 4th edition, edited by Robert S. Goodhart and Maurice E. Shils (Lea & Febiger, 1968); and *Nutrition in a Nutshell* by Roger J. Williams (Doubleday, 1962). However, it is best to get a direct dietary consultation.

There are reports that, if both the exercise and the dietary aspects of the program are applied, all the above chronic conditions are benefited. The most difficult one to treat is obesity. Blood pressure has been returned to normal, the severity of the diabetes has been reduced in some patients to the point where medication isn't necessary, and there is some evidence that the progression of atherosclerosis has been stopped. In 1975 Nathan Pritikin completed a controlled research study which indicates that atherosclerosis can be stopped and even reversed. His diet consists of 10 percent fats, 10 percent protein and 80 percent complex carbohydrates. Pritikin feels that "99 percent of heart disease can be prevented" with this diet and with exercise. The interesting aspect of this study is that vessels already clogged with atherosclerotic plaques can be reopened. It is an exciting development in medicine and should be closely watched.

Once again, no one with the above diseases should begin any program of exercise and diet without the full approval and help of his physician and close consultation with a dietitian, and only after a thorough stress test.

UNANSWERED QUESTIONS

This form of running therapy is not going to eliminate mental illness, but I believe that it will take its place as a useful form of therapy. However, many questions arise that need to be explored. For example, is it the change in cerebral blood flow that engineers the changes? Or is it the stimulus to the lower brain centers? How is it possible to identify clearly factors such as the enthusiasm of the therapists who believe in the procedure? For we know that this is often the critical factor. Do the changes last over a period of years? If we compare it to other diseases, are we speaking of a five-year cure rate or an absolute cure? Perhaps such questions as these are irrelevant and others which relate to the state of one's soul are more appropriate.

At any rate it is clear to me that this is a distinct form of psychotherapy. People dreamed for all of recorded history before Freud and Jung finally discovered meaning and utilitarian, therapeutic use in the dreams of their patients. Man has been running for perhaps three million years and only very recently has he become sedentary. Dreams were discussed as esoteric and irrelevant in our modern scientific age. And long-distance running has been misidentified as a sport, with the usual nonsense of heroes and competition placing a minor barrier over the physical and mental benefits that lie beneath the visible activity.

The joggers have been equally treated with wry amusement as harmless, tottering characters who could do as well with their time sitting in front of the TV set with a beer in hand. And finally, the marathoners have been labeled a group of fanatics and perhaps lunatics, who have been especially endowed by nature with superlative legs, lungs and hearts, and therefore were not at all like the rest of mankind.

We do need to look behind these stereotypes. I feel that slow long-distance running is not a sport at all. It is an activity that resonates with our biological heritage. And, in so resonating, we may be able to penetrate the confines of our circumstance and establish a better harmony with ourselves and the world. And I feel that cardiovascular disease is abnormal. Just about every normally healthy child could be helped (not trained) to run a marathon.* It is not unreasonable to think this way when adults who have had heart attacks and open heart surgery have finished marathons. We will then be able to begin a true inner revolution in our culture. Running is a simple process, natural and normal. To place this fundamental health-inducing tool in the hands of virtually every child may help us eliminate our number-one killer and crippler. In addition, it may also help each individual open new doors into his own soul.

ADDICTION

Slow long-distance running is addictive. I mean this in a medical way. We say something is addictive when (1) it produces a desire or need in the user to increase the dosage, and (2) deprivation produces in the user adverse physical effects known as withdrawal symptoms. A knowledgeable junkie in the good old days of the 1960's, with multiple drug programs to help him, found that he had to plan to sign up periodically in various programs to reduce the cost of his habit. The waiting lists were so long that upon discharge from Program A the junkie would immediately sign up for Program B. If busted along the way, he would then have proof that he was trying to help himself, having signed up for Program B. He went from program to program, enduring the pangs of withdrawal each time, because of the cost of his ever-increasing doses; upon discharge from program A or B, he could get away with a lowered dose, and when, as time progressed, the cost of the habit increased until he finally had to be cut back again, he could enter—or reenter—Program B or A.

---

* Editor's note: Dr. Kostrubala began a marathon program at St. Charles Grammar School in San Diego in April, 1975. By the end of May, 1975, twenty-three children had completed a 20-kilometer race. By December, 1975, six had completed a full marathon. This is the first known marathoning grammar school in history.

Slow long-distance running does not function exactly like an opiate addiction, nor is it identical with an alcohol or barbiturate addiction. It does have some similarities to the use of hallucinogens such as LSD, mescaline and hashish. The best way to clarify all these is to compare them. The comparative data I will use are simple. First I'll compare the withdrawal effects. And I'll also stick to a few well-known drugs: alcohol, opiates, barbiturates and hallucinogens. I'll also compare the time it takes to become addicted to each, the effect upon the mind with each drug and the curious social phenomena associated with them. (The hallucinogens are not considered addictive, but, in their effect, they warrant comparison here both with the other drugs named and with running.)

Let's start with alcohol. The reason alcohol is such a uniquely destructive drug is that it is equally miscible with water. Where water goes, alcohol goes. Into every cell. No blood-brain barrier to protect the central nervous system. Its toxicity is directly related to the dose. People can and do kill themselves outright by drinking too much booze too fast. It usually occurs in some silly circumstance where the person challenges someone else to a competition based on their drinking ability. Alcohol's major withdrawal symptom is the medical emergency delirium tremens. People die with DT's. The slow effects are the ones we know best. They lead to social deterioration via subtle brain damage. Evidences of addiction are: (1) wanting more to drink, and (2) showing signs of withdrawal when one can't have it (we call it the shakes). Alcohol is socially accepted and even encouraged. It produces and is part of cultural conformity. We are a drinking nation. Just pay attention to some of the ads that try to reach our senses—in one, if we drink such and such a beer, we automatically have "gusto" in our lives. In another, we are in the pristine beauty of "sky-blue waters."

In opiate addiction, including heroin, the withdrawal symptoms aren't too bad. The individual will suffer somewhat from complete withdrawal, but with the use of another opiate such as methadone, the withdrawal is easier. Opiates usually produce an inner sense of calm and peace, a feeling of comfortable detachment where one feels inwardly observant but relaxed. Often it's like having a cushion all around you, a soft barrier to the external world and a cessation of all inner anxiety. Some have called it an orgasm of the gastrointestinal tract. One social phenomenon of heroin addicts is that they are conformists. They play cops-and-robbers and all the other inner-circle games of buying, dealing, stealing and use that are involved. We the public are really turned on by all this. The events of *The French Connection* are all part of the same dull old cops-robbers, maybe social-protest jazzy scene. Junkies do look alike and eventually act alike. I'm not talking about the thrill user—the middle-classer who gets his vicarious jollies by the thrill of it all—I'm talking about the real user, like the real runner.

A barbiturate is a "downer," causing a reduction in attention to the outer and inner world. One withdrawal symptom can be death from seizures. The social aspect is very important. With barbiturates, whatever happens is what people expect to happen, from active violence to sleep. Again, these individuals conform to the culture. They, too, play a cops-and-robbers game, but not as intensely as do the opiate users.

The users of hallucinogens are very conforming. They usually move toward a cultistic aspect of their use. They have leaders like the tragic Dr. Timothy Leary. Cops-and-robbers is a heavy thing with them. And they spin off a high percentage of nonsense, also. The conformity is like the conformity of a monastery. The monks are all alike, but quite different from the society around them.

Running doesn't work exactly like these drugs. The pattern, however, is addiction. One can become addicted to running within a few months. Usually it takes longer. If someone is able to get out and run daily, or at least five days a week for an hour each time at 75 percent of his maximum cardiac output, then the addiction will settle in a lot earlier than at three times per week. The withdrawal symptoms of the slow long-distance runner occur when he is forced to stop running. This happened to me. I got the flu, and a nasty case of it. It mystified both me and my physicians. It got bad enough that they put me in the hospital for five days to test me out—to see if the lab data could find anything that they were missing. Well, they ended up telling me that, after all, it did seem to be the flu bug everyone else was getting—and advised me to reduce my running.

I was weak and shaky, but the sense of anxiety I developed was unbelievable. I just had to run. As soon as I could, I tried to run. I wobbled about, got sicker and had to return to bed. Back in bed I was worse off. I had insomnia then. I'd toss and turn. My body ached to be outside to work out—to be able to pour the sweat off. And I couldn't. The flu slowly gave up its hold on my ears, nose, throat and lungs and left me weakened and wasted.

Even more devastating was my clear observation that my body was getting back to its untrained flabby condition. I had gained 10 pounds. I had the same diet, but less exercise. I was afraid to diet because I was fearful that dieting might cut down my recovery rate. Briefly, I knew how to be well and healthy—I did not know how to be sick.

The comparison between slow long-distance running and hallucinogens is fairly close. Running, as described in this book, does produce an altered state of consciousness. A nonordinary avenue of perception does seem to open up .The runner is changed by this experience. Most important of all, he remembers his experience and is able to judge later on whether his insight is a truly valid one or not. The experience is something like a dream. We may not be able to understand it and may only be able to guess at some of the symbolism that is brought to our consciousness. It may be beneficial or it may be filed away in memory as a piece of a puzzle to be worked in later. The slow long-distance runner experiences a part of his unconscious. It is an altered state of consciousness.

Here is another valid comparison. After running slow long distances, there is often a complete relief of tension and anxiety. The runner is washed out from within. This is quite similar to using heroin. After a run, runners often feel quite loose and sometimes a bit silly. There is a lot of easy flow going on in groups.

These comparisons show the similarities of slow long-distance running to the addictive drugs named and to the hallucinogens. However, all these drugs, whether frowned upon by society or subtly supported (as in alcohol addiction), produce behavior which can best be described as conformity. The major difference in slow long-distance running as addictive is that its withdrawal symptoms are primarily insomnia and anxiety. But the most striking social aspect of this addiction is that, far from producing conformity, it seems to promote individuality.

9

Marathon

I KNOW THE MARATHON is impossible. It is impossible physically and spiritually. I am afraid of it. I can't drive the course ahead of time in a car. It's too long. No one can run that far. Two years ago I couldn't run 100 yards. I was fat. I still feel fat. I think fat. The scale says I weigh 175 pounds. I see 230. I feel 300.

It is 6:30 A.M., December 15, 1974. The Honolulu Marathon. It is still dark. The sun is down in the east, its glow hidden by the edge of the earth. Soon it will rise out of the Pacific but for a while it will be hidden from me by Diamond Head. For a while. I say a silent prayer for a cloud cover. Heat will ruin me. Humidity, heat and torrid winds are all dangers; external dangers—not those of mind. Those unknown factors in my heart, legs and soul, those are the barriers toward which I am running. And, which, of course, are insurmountable. (The marathon is impossible.)

The gun goes off—what a sense of relief. The whole horrible thing has started. I am running into the dim light. Cops on motorcycles with blue lights are guarding us. Jesus! What a mob. There are three hundred of us. All ages. Twelve to sixty-eight. Women and girls. Men and boys. I wonder if I will finish. I wonder if anyone will die. I feel rotten as I begin. I am tired. Heavy. Soon my right knee begins to hurt. A stabbing pain in the right outside kneecap. It sends a chill of fear into me. Am I injured? I have felt that pain—or one like it, I can't clearly remember—once before. I continue to run. I look at my watch. Twenty minutes gone. I feel I should quit. I am going to hurt myself. Now both legs below the knee begin to hurt. The aching of bruised muscle. Is my body rebelling? Only a masochist would go on. I could limp and quit. But I begin to find glory in the pain.

As I run, I feel the whole of me working. My body has to be alive. It has to work. My heart surges ahead. My legs hurt, but I am dancing a special dance of life. Somehow, I am glorifying life, defying death in all it's forms. Right in the snapping teeth of death, I dance and laugh. Knowing in a vague yet entirely wonderful way that this is the way I give honor and glory to God. The jaws of death will get me, eventually. When they do, I will go fighting all the way. I know this is the way. I suspect, somehow, that this is also related to the peace and living forever afterward. It is life to life. Death is the enemy now to both my body and my soul. Afterward it is just to my soul.

Twenty-five minutes have gone by. We run through Waikiki. Past amazed shopkeepers who are just opening up. I recall my pains. They have all gone. The sun is really rising now. The healing sun. The arc of the day. The beginning. My life is beginning. What past? It is now, only now. The sun, the dawn. I'm running. I am new—born a million years old.

I have to pee. My bladder feels full. But I can't find anyplace to go. Feel silly. How the hell can I solve this? I call out to Fred, a friend from home who is here to see the marathon and to attend the meetings of the American Medical Joggers Association. He is pacing me on a bike, feeding me fluids along the way. I tell him I have to pee. It is one of those idiot communications. How can he help? What I want is sympathy. He does his job, something like a sympathetic shake of the head. It does help. I find a bush, get behind it. And pee. Wow! I feel lighter.

I'm scared. Seem so alone. Nice to have the days. Not cold now. I feel warm. No aches or pains. Got to remember to slow down. Go too fast and it won't work. But I feel like sprinting a bit (a sprint for me is really a faster jog). I am beginning to feel great. We are running through a neighborhood. Up toward Diamond Head. My speed increases. Up ahead is a little kid. Barefoot and no shirt. Glasses. Very slight of frame. A really neat runner. We run together. He is twelve years old. This is his first marathon. His dad and older brother are ahead. His mom drives along, giving each of them fluids. I begin to have one of those powerful emotions that come over me when running slow long distances. I have the rising up of all the emotions of a proud, loving father. I want to reach over and hug that kid. I want to tell him that I think he is the best son a father could have. All the good feelings, all the pride and the love I have felt for my sons, are focused like the rays of the sun by a magnifying glass into a burning, intense, bright emotion. I love that boy. I am so damn proud of him.

Then two other men come along. In their fifties. I begin to feel tired. I begin to slow up. One hour and fifteen minutes have gone. The boy and the two men pass me. I force myself to keep up. I don't want to fall behind them, so I push myself and get ahead. Maybe five steps or so. They probably think I am competing, because they pass me, then I pass them and pull ahead, but I am only afraid. We go to and fro that way. They catch up and then I pull away. The wind is heavy. Fear and fatigue are on me.

Suddenly, it seems, we are in a residential neighborhood. Shady lawns. Green leaves. Fred is there on the

bike and I feel really good again. In fact, I feel too
good. I have a running high on. I feel I can fly. I know
that if I'm to finish I can't let myself go. Just ahead,
maybe two blocks, are three young marines. In USMC
shirts. They are yelling, cheering themselves on. All between eighteen and twenty-one years of age. I am near
them at the wrong time—for all of us. Those three kids
make me angry. They don't respect the horror of this
race. They are loud. They run in unison. In step. In
cadence. Marathoners, when they run, are quiet. They
respect. They know the fear. They know what's ahead.
These kids are bragging. They have hubris. And me?
Well, I am the offended god. All of my male competitive drive is unleashed. The civilized veneer is off. I
motion to Fred: "See those bums? I'm gonna get them.
Watch." Fred looks astonished. Who is this guy? A
road-running Frankenstein? A marathoning Mr. Hyde?
Mr. Fat and Forty-four disappears. The Head Ape
comes out. The Alpha Male. Time swirls into the past.
The clan is endangered by these kids—they have to be
told, have to be put down.

I accelerate smoothly right up to them. I come in
casual. I ask, "Hey, you guys in the Corps?" As if I
can't see or read. One answers, "Yes, sir," in that
special mock-servile tone I know so well. I answer,
"Gee, that's neat. I was in the Corps in 1950. Guess
that was before you were born." And before they can
answer, I floor my accelerator. My speed picks up and
I fly away from them. I am gliding effortlessly—delighted—and proud of what I've done.

I forget it soon enough. I have to pay for my burst
of energy and my aggression. The road is long. The
sun is up. Heat comes on. Head down a bit. Shorter
steps. It really feels good. It isn't hard. My chest is
whamming away. My heart is really working. I'm not
afraid of it. Good heart, work hard. Burning in throat,
still going. God, I'm slow. Keep up. The center is forged
by acts of will. Like a giant hammer it drives the stuff
of the periphery into the tight hard core. It is round,

pounded, silver white and begins to glow from the many, many blows that gives it its life, and its shape.

Its glow is soft—silver. It becomes denser—and as the stuff of which it's made grows closer, it becomes harder and harder to keep it round, shining, glowing.

Fatigue builds. Will is not enough. Finally, the question of why enters and the blows weaken, are fewer.

The center holds itself for a while. To fail means death. The center then comes apart. Bursting or oozing. Back again to the periphery.

A counterattack is mustered by the powers of will. A new pounding. A second glowing. But then a greater final fatigue enters.

It ends. There isn't anything left. Why is left unanswered, unheard.

Time passes somehow. I take fluids. Yell at the people in the gardens to get their hoses out and sprinkle the runners if they want to be sprinkled. They all seem to laugh. They don't know how good that feels. At the timing stations I see I can't beat 3½ hours. I am slow. The race people are really nice, giving me fluids, time and encouragement.

Suddenly, coming along the way back, I see the front four. They are like gods. They run the race at a pace—5 minutes per mile—that I have never run in my life. I had heard Ken Moore speak the day before. He is ahead, elbow to elbow with another guy. They have about 10 miles to go and they are flying, straining, fighting for the lead. He is ahead. I also heard Frank Shorter talk and spoke to him briefly. He is fourth. Frank's face is drawn, but he is running gracefully and smoothly.

The Abo hunts—sees kangaroo. Runs after kangaroo. Abo slow, like me, but steady. Kangaroo spurts on. All day. Tortoise and hare. Sun beats down. All day, Abo goes. Night falls. Abo sleeps. Kangaroo sleeps. Dawn and Abo gets up. Goes over to kangaroo. Kangaroo can't move. Too stiff. A marsupial. Not like

Abo. Not like me. A runner. Abo kills kangaroo. Then carries kangaroo back all day. I can do it too.

Shoulders a little stiff. Roll 'em around. At mile 15 I hear heavy footsteps behind me. I turn and see a short Japanese gaining on me. His legs seem bowed. He looks like he is struggling with every step. He hits the ground with the front outside of his foot. He has on a fatigue cap. It looks like a Japanese Army cap. Visions of World War II come back. All the old movies. The old memories. I was eleven years old on December 7, 1941. I recall it all vividly. I say, he won't catch me. I keep on. The sponges with water in them at the aid stations cool my head. The fluids are a godsend. Sweat pours off. At 18 miles I hear him again, right behind me. I pull away. At 19 miles he pulls up even with me. To my right. He says "Hi, I'm Larry. I'm from here. Thanks for pacing me." I introduce myself. He and I chat a second and then he says: "You helped me pace all the time. Can I help you? Maybe I can pick you up." By that he means a kind of moral support, a lift, a pacing, that helps break fatigue, gets one through to the other side where it's easy again. I say, "Sure. Thanks a lot." And I try to stay with him. We go through the 20-mile checkpoint, 21 miles, 22 miles. At 22½ miles I can't stay with him. By then I love him. He is fifty-seven years old and this is his first marathon. As he leaves me and disappears ahead, I am very, very proud of him. God, what a man. Dripping sweat, being polite, driving himself, helping me. I cry for him, small wet tears. Happy tears. Grateful.

I recall the marines and wonder what they think. The moral issues are balled up. A mixed knot. Another gift from this marathon.

I am so jazzed by our culture. Radio, TV, movies, competition, Rah-rah, motorcycles, autos, airplanes, roaring music. I am addicted. I can make more noise in my head, in my soul, by booze, coffee, relationships, work. Lots of things help make my soul, a mixed, noisy, racket. A clanging caldron of noise color, lights.

It is impossible to find peace. My soul, poisoned, detaches itself from my body. My body responds by poisoning itself. Fat accumulates.

Somehow in the running I find the way to let my natural body take over. "It," not me, begins to correct my excesses—"it" begins to demand quietness. I even find running at 5:00 A.M. a joy—dark and silent, even frightening. I am finding my soul in the middle of an insane asylum.

I find it is a duty to write about my experiences. I am afraid of my terrible tendency to try to force others to find what I am only beginning to discover.

My back hurts. Old burning pain, right side, lower back. Concentrate on it. It's going away. There, gone.

At 23 miles a woman pulls up to me from behind. It is a woman I met at the talks in the previous two days. She is thirty-seven years old. This is her first marathon. We are facing the Diamond Head hill. She asks me to pace her. I had run hills. She is fearful of hills. I grab inside for some energy, find it and push up the hills. I feel I am pulling her along. We crest them and she has lots of energy left. She pulls ahead, finishes well ahead of me. And she takes second place in the Women's Division. I am happy for her. She looks beautiful while running. Smooth, young, graceful.

I am somewhere around the 25-mile mark. All I can think of is finishing. In spite of the fatigue, the beauty of the Pacific Ocean to my left comes through to me. I know that I can finish. I am over Diamond Head and it is downhill now to the Kapiolani Park finish line.

Each time I go onto the track, I am able to recall bits and pieces of the fear and pain that went before. I often wonder if I am somewhere in the middle. Perhaps a year or two from now, the pain and the fear will be as great again. I don't see how they can.

As I run, I recall previous runs, previous pain, earlier marathons. Little bits and pieces come into me again. I hope I have exhumed the want. Perhaps not. Dying may be something like this. I hope it is. I would like to die like Zorba, screaming and fighting to live. It's my dedication to life. To all life. Somehow, I am too Western. I like the word "occidental." I hate the word "amorphous." I want to be me, forever. As I understand this idea, it is very Christian, very orthodox, very Catholic.

Genesis may mean an elevation away from the swamping miasma of the mob. I hope it does. I vote for it. For that party. If that is so, then perhaps we can build immortality. Then the slogan works. Immortality is an act of the will.

There are crowds of people the last mile on either side. No one knows me, but they applaud as I finish. They do that for everyone. God, it feels great! I am all alone. My back straightens and I feel lighter and I come into the finish smiling, actually grinning. At the last 200 yards I begin to sprint. God knows where I get this energy, but it all feels right.

My feelings are so strong these last 200 yards that I begin to choke up, to feel that inner urge to cry. Like a little kid. I know I can't do that; maybe I can, but it would look odd. All these emotions come boiling up and then, before I know it, I cross the finish line in the crowd of other finishers, their families and friends.

I have finished: I have won.

Someone congratulates me. It is a blur. I get a can of Primo Beer in my hand. My legs hurt and I am stiff and even that pain and stiffness feels good. It helps keep the memory of that race alive. Everyone talks, congratulates everyone else. People drink beer and the award ceremonies begin.

Finally, there is a pause in the noise and action. A crowd is running in. Six hours have passed since we started and the last man is finishing. He is a sixty-eight-year-old native Hawaiian. Everyone smiles, cheers, takes his picture. This is his first marathon. Everyone is proud of him. We are all him. The awards ceremonies continue. There are many trophies. For men of various ages, kids and women. But at one time, twenty-two men get up on that stage. They are all dressed in black sweats with small white trim. Black, the color of death. They are from thirty to sixty years of age. They are very erect and very quiet. They come from Canada, Hawaii and the other states. Those from Canada have an interesting insignia on their T-shirts. It is a red broken heart. We in the crowd know what that means, who they are. We stand up, tired as we are. Each one of these men finished this marathon. And each one of these men had once had a heart attack. We can only guess what this moment means to them. They had been there, at the edge of this life. They had been hit by the disease that kills more American men than any other disease. They had faced our number-one killer. And now they are in a new category. Many of us know an odd but strangely powerful fact. That fact is that there has never been a proved death reported from coronary disease, a heart attack, in anyone who has finished a marathon within seven years after finishing. Are these men now protected as we are? We pray they are, for their sakes. And for ours.

There are not too many people in the United States who have finished a marathon. Out of a population of over 200 million, perhaps 5,000 will have finished a marathon in 1975. Those 5,000 are really ordinary people. They come from all areas of life—young, old, male, female, rich, poor, bright, dull, even some who have had heart attacks. I keep remembering my Uncle Frank. He died of a coronary. He was in his fifties. I loved him. I know that if he had known about the marathon and that it could protect him from a cruelly premature death, he would have loved to train and run it. He would be alive today had he known. He was a man who spread kindness and a soft joy about him. It's been seventeen years since he died and I still miss him.

I wonder how many other men and women are dying needlessly just because they do not know that they can do something to protect themselves.

Bibliography

Anderson, E. D., MB MANZCP. "Psychological Aspects of the Course at Outward Bound." *NZ Med J,* November 1972.

Baekeland, F. "Exercise Deprivation, Sleep and Psychological Reactions." *Arch Gen Psychiat* 22, April 1970.

———, and Lasky, R. "Exercise and Sleep Patterns in College Athletes." *Percep Mot Skills* 23 (1966): 1203-7.

Bassler, T., and Scaff, J. "Letter: Can I Avoid Heart-Attack?" *Lancet* 1 (862): 863-64, May 1974.

Brunner, B. C. "Personality and Motivating Factors Influencing Adult Participation in Vigorous Physical Activity." *Res Quart* 40:464-469, October 1969.

Byrd, O. E. "Reilef of Tension by Exercise: Survey of Medical Viewpoints and Practices." *J Sch Health* 33:238-39, May 1963.

Clement, F. J. "Longitudinal and Cross-Sectional Assessments of Age Changes in Physical Strength as

Related to Sex, Social Class, and Mental Ability." *J Gerontol* 29(4):423-29, July 1974.

Collingwood, T. R. "The Effects of Physical Training upon Behavior and Self Attitudes." *J Clin Psych* 28:283-85, October 1972.

Cooper, K. H. *Aerobics.* New York: Bantam Books, Inc., 1968.

Dencker, S. J. "Physical Training." *Scand J Rehab Med* 3 (1971):57-60.

Dwyer, J. T.; Blonde, C. V.; and Mayer, J. "Treating Obesity in Growing Children. 2. Specific Aspects: Activity and Diet." *Postgrad Med* 51(7):111-15, June 1972.

Fink, M.; Taylor, M.A.; and Volavka, J. "Anxiety Precipitated by Lactate." Letter to the Editor, *New Eng J Med* 281:1429, 18 December 1969.

Friedman, E. H. "Personality Types and Coronary Artery Disease." Letter to the Editor, *JAMA* 219:385, 1972.

Goldsmith, R., and Hale, T. "Relationship Between Habitual Physical Activity and Physical Fitness." *Amer J Clin Nutr* 24(12): 1489-93, December 1971.

Gore, I. Y. "Physical Activity and Aging—A Survey of Soviet Literature. 3. The Character of Physical Activity; Training and Longitudinal Results." *Gerontol Clin* (Basel) 14(2) (1972): 78-85.

Guthrie, D., and Vivian, G. "The Effect of Jogging on Physical Fitness and Self-Concept in Hospitalized Alcoholics." *Quart J Stud Alc* 33:1073-78, December 1972.

Hammer, W. M., and Wilmore, J. H. "An Exploratory Investigation in Personality Measures and Physiological Alterations During a 10-Week Jogging Program." *J Sports Med Phys Fitness* 13(4):238-47, December 1973.

Hanson, J. S., and Nedde, W. H. "Long-Term Physical Training Effect in Sedentary Females." *J Appl Physiol* 37(1):112-16, July 1974.

Harris, D. V. "Physical Activity History and Attitudes of Middle-Aged Men." *Med Sci Sports* 2(4):203-8, Winter 1970.

Harris, M. B., and Hallbauer, E. S. "Self-Directed Weight Control Through Eating and Exercise." *Behav Res Ther* 11(4):523-29, November 1973.

Hartley, L. H.; Mason, J. W.; Hogan, R. P. Jones, L. G.; Kotchen, T. A.; Mougey, E. H.; Wherry, F. E.; Pennington, L. L.; and Ricketts, P. T. "Multiple Hormonal Responses to Prolonged Exercise in Relation to Physical Training." *J. Appl Physiol* 33:607-10, November 1972.

———, "Multiple Hormonal Responses to Graded Exercise in Relation to Physical Conditioning." *J Appl Physiol* 3(1972):602-6.

Heinzelmann, F., and Gabley, R. "Response to Physical Activity Programs and Their Effects on Health Behavior." *Pub Health Rep* 85(10)(1970):905-11.

Hobson, J. A. "Sleep After Exercise." *Science* 162 (1968):1503-5.

Hunter, W. M.; Foneseka, C. C.; Passmore, R. "Growth Hormone: Important Role in Muscular Exercise in Adults." *Science* 150(1965):1051.

Ismail, A. H., and Trachtman, L. E. "Jogging the Imagination." *Psychology Today*, March 1973, pp. 79-82.

Kavanagh, T.; Shephard, R. J.; and Doney, H. "Hypnosis and Exercise: A Possible Combined Therapy Following Myocardial Infarction." *Amer J Clin Hypn* 16(3):160-65, January 1974.

Lefin, H., and Simon, P. "Improvement of the Intellectual and Spiritual Condition of the Aged Patients by Kinesitherapy." *Brux Med* 53(2):93-96, February 1973.

Massie, J. F., and Shephard, R. J. "Physiological and Psychological Effects of Training—A Comparison of Individual and Gymnasium Programs, with a

Characterization of the Exercise 'Drop-Out.' " *Med Sci Sports* 3(3):110-17, Fall 1971.

Morgan, W. P. "Physical Fitness and Emotional Health: A Review." *Amer Correct Ther J* 23:124–27.

————; Roberts, J. A.; Brand, F. R.; and Feinerman, A. D. "Psychological Effect of Chronic Physical Activity." *Med Sci Sports* 2(4):213-17, Winter 1970.

Murphy, J. B.; Bennett, R. N.; Martin, R. C.; and Hagen, J. M. "Studies in the Relationship of Physical Fitness and Mental Adjustment" *Amer Correct Ther J* 26(2):50-51, March-April 1972.

Orwin, A. " 'The Running Treatment': A Preliminary Communication on a New Use for an Old Therapy (Physical Activity) in the Agoraphobic Syndrome." *Brit J Psychiat* 122(567):175-79, February 1973.

Penman, K. A. Hastad, D. N.; and Cords, W. L. "Success of the Authoritarian Coach." *J Soc Psychol* 92(1):155-56, February 1974.

Pitts, F. N., and McClure, J. N. "Lactate Metabolism in Anxiety Neurosis." *New Eng J Med* 277:1329-36, 21 December 1967.

Rahe, R. H.; Tuffli, C. F.; Suchor, R. J.; and Ransom, J. A. "Group Therapy in the Outpatient Management of Post-Myocardial Infarction Patients." *Psychiatry in Medicine* 4(1):77-88, 1973.

Rode, A., and Shephard, R. J. "Fitness of the Canadian Eskimo—The Influence of Season." *Med Sci Sports* 5(3):170-73, Fall 1973.

Roth, W. T. "Some Motivational Aspects of Exercise." *J Sports Med Phys Fitness* 14(1):40-47, March 1974 .

Rushall, B. S. "The Status of Personality Research and Application in Sports and Physical Education." *J Sports Med Phys Fitness* 13(4):218-90, December 1973.

Secord, P. F., and Jourard, S. M. "The Appraisal of

Body Cathexis; Bodycathexis and the Self." *J Cons Psychol* 17 (1953):343-47.

Shephard, R. J. "World Health Standards of Cardio-respiratory Performance." *Arch Environ Health* 13 (1966):664-72.

Stanaway, R. G., and Hullin, R. P. "The Relationship of Exercise Response to Personality." *Psychol Med* 3(3):343-49, August 1973.

Tillman, K. "Relationship Between Physical Fitness and Selected Personality Traits." *Res Quart* 36 (1965):483-89.

Weil, A. *The Natural Mind: A New Way of Looking at Drugs and the Higher Consciousness.* Boston: Houghton Mifflin Co., 1972.

Wendt, D. T., and Patterson, T. W. "Personality Characteristics of Women in Intercollegiate Competition." *Percep Mot Skills* 38(3):861-62, June 1974.

Wiesner, R. R., and Sharkey, B. J. "Some Characteristics of Wilderness Backpackers." *Percep Mot Skills* 36(1973):876-78.

Wunderlich, R. A.; Kenrick, M.; Pearce, M.; Lozes, J.; and Ball, M. F. "Psychological Considerations in Physical Therapy for Obese Patients." *Phy Ther* 53(7):757-61, July 1973.